Simple Habits of Exceptional (But Not Perfect) Parents

Ken Dolan-Del Vecchio

ISBN: 0692068287
ISBN 13: 9780692068281
GreenGate Leadership, LLC,
Palmer, Massachusetts

Cover art by Christina Dolan-Del Vecchio

Cover image by Photography by Duval

Praise for *Simple Habits of Exceptional (But Not Perfect) Parents*

In *Simple Habits of Exceptional (But Not Perfect) Parents*, author Ken Dolan-Del Vecchio draws from his extensive clinical and organizational consulting background to provide a first-rate, exceptionally comprehensive manual for parents striving to help their children thrive in today's challenging world. Ken covers topics that we, as parents, face with great regularity—giving advice, negotiating boundaries, conveying respect, fostering self-esteem, and most importantly, cultivating joy. These are the tasks of daily living for parents but can often get lost in our hectic lives, our digitally connected world and our desire to see our children achieve—but at what cost? This highly practical book is a refreshing reminder of what is most essential in parenting—a loving approach to helping our children become who they are meant to be.

—Brad Harrington, EdD; Executive Director, Boston College Center for Work & Family

Habits are the social messengers by which parents instill values and behaviors in their children. Ken Dolan-Del Vecchio provides receptive parents with practical, useful means by which to influence how their children will love, handle conflict, appreciate differences, ask for help, mind their health and mental health and much more. The greatest gift we can give our children is to help them surpass us, and this book shows how.

—Lloyd I. Sederer, MD; Medical Editor for Mental Health, *The Huffington Post*; Adjunct Professor, Columbia/Mailman School of Public Health

Simple Habits of Exceptional (But Not Perfect) Parents by Ken Dolan-Del Vecchio is an easy-to-understand guide, almost an instruction manual, which can help you navigate the 3 a.m. inconsolable cries, out-of-the blue questions about where babies come from, sibling bickering and other challenges we parents face. The book is filled with real-life examples, stories that make the issues and the author's advice come alive, and each chapter ends with helpful summary points. Goethe wrote, "There are two things children should get from their parents: roots and wings." This book will help you give your child both.

—Jorge R. Petit, MD; NYS Regional Senior VP, Beacon Health Options

Inspiring, hopeful, and chock full of terrific ideas, Ken Dolan-Del Vecchio's *Simple Habits of Exceptional (But Not Perfect) Parents* shares practical wisdom that will help parents from their child's early years through adulthood.

—Monica McGoldrick, MSW, PhD (h.c.); Director, Multicultural Family Institute and author of *You Can Go Home Again*

Immediately valuable, *Simple Habits of Exceptional (But Not Perfect) Parents* provides readers with a trove of practical skills for the vast array of issues parents traverse with their children. Ken Dolan-Del Vecchio is the master of offering friendly and compassionate wisdom for people in relationships. His sense of humor and willingness to share his own personal challenges with parenting renders this a joyful and satisfying read.

—Lynn Parker, MSW, PhD; Professor Emeriti, University of Denver, Graduate School of Social Work; Family therapist in private practice

Family therapist, health and wellness executive, and writer Dolan-Del Vecchio (*The Pet Loss Companion*, 2013, etc.) offers common-sense parenting advice.

The author expands upon the traditional adage that children are a gift by averring that parents can also be gifts to their children—that is, if they're attentive, caring parents. He expounds upon this idea over the course of five chapters, exploring different types of habits ("Habits of Heart and Mind," "People Habits," "Spiritual Habits," and "Healthy Habits") and concluding with a discussion of "Reflections and Rewards." Each chapter is divided into titled sections, with a list of the most important points at the end of each. Throughout the book, Dolan-Del Vecchio emphasizes another theme: that parents should develop "power with" rather than "power over" their children. The latter, as the name suggests, is about dominance and control, while "power with" emphasizes doing the best for both parent and offspring. The author writes from his own experience as a father and a family therapist, backing up his suggestions with examples and stories, including details from his private life that make him a more relatable adviser: "While I want to consistently show love, I have also caught myself letting my attention drift, impatiently, when Erik needed a listening ear." In general, he advocates a compassionate, gentle style of parenting, with a strong emphasis on simply being present for one's kids. He also notes that parents should not beat themselves up over past mistakes but rather learn from them and move forward. Another key point is that one should accept a child's uniqueness instead of trying to mold him or her into an ideal. Dolan-Del Vecchio writes in a very clear, straightforward style, eschewing unfamiliar jargon. The deliberately short sections, despite their presence in very long chapters, make the book easy to read, and the bullet points and summaries effectively reinforce important ideas. The author also avoids overusing pithy quotations from other experts, but he does use a few very effectively—particularly one from the late Fred Rogers of *Mister Rogers' Neighborhood*.

Expertly crafted parenting advice that advocates gentleness and presence above all else.

—Kirkus Reviews

For Erik, Christina, Tim, Lynn and Laura

Think about how you want your kids to
remember this time 20 years from now.
—Monica McGoldrick,
family therapist and author

Contents

Introduction

Simple and Not So Simple

We are the holders of a priceless gift, a gift we received from countless generations we never knew, a gift that only we now possess and only we can give to our children. That unique gift, of course, is the gift of ourselves.

—Fred Rogers

Imagine a world in which parents receive every child as a miraculous gift, a new human being at once fragile and full of potential to live a wonderful life—if we provide the care that will help them make it happen. While almost any adult can help bring a child into being, only a parent in the truest sense recognizes their child as such a gift. And only an *exceptional* parent sees, as Fred Rogers reminds us, that they, in turn, may become their child's most precious gift.

An exceptional parent knows that raising a child isn't so much about buying toys, expensive vacations and the like, but about giving their time and attention. Exceptional parents help their children feel loved and valued. They teach integrity and grit by example and through the honesty with which they provide guidance and share their personal stories. They instill in their child the faith that she or he was born for a life of joy, loving relationships and rewarding adventures. An exceptional parent is a gift every day.

Now, lest you think that exceptional parenting is as unattainable as finding the Holy Grail, my years as family therapist, coach, father, son and human being have taught me something encouraging: exceptional parenting doesn't spring from genius, Mother

Theresa-like saintliness, or any other superhuman quality. Instead, it emerges from simple, conscious habits. It comes into being when you remember the power you wield in your child's life and act accordingly, showing that you value your child's strengths and interests, supporting rather than undermining your child's positive feelings about himself or herself, and allowing your child their mistakes and the opportunities to learn from them.

Ironically, our most important parenting habits stretch beyond those that directly provide love and guidance to our children. I am speaking here of the behaviors that demonstrate our own positive values, effective ways of interacting with the world around us, and successful navigation of the unforeseen challenges life throws our way. All of our habits have far-reaching significance for our children because they look to us as a guiding example. In fact, we will always stand among our child's most influential role models.

While habits of exceptional parenting may be simple to grasp, they're not always easy to practice. When I recently advised a mother and father to let their 14-year-old son manage his own homework rather than supervise him as they'd previously been doing, they understood that allowing him to take responsibility for his work made sense. Yet they resisted doing so.

"What if he loses all self-confidence, decides that he's stupid, and stops trying to learn?"

"What if he tosses his homework aside, fails ninth grade, and starts talking about quitting school when he turns sixteen?"

"What if he becomes depressed and suicidal?"

Such fears often confront us at the threshold of change. Other obstacles can also get in the way: entrenched habits running on autopilot, time pressure that makes it seem easier to stick with the familiar, and uncertainty about how to go about doing what is new. When it comes to trying out a different behavior, *simple to understand* rarely means *simple to do*.

This book identifies exceptional parenting habits that you can learn and offers guidance on how to make them your own. Your children will benefit greatly. They stand to gain self-esteem, belief in their own competence, respect for themselves and others, a compelling vision for their future, and the determination to work hard toward their goals. They will develop the capacity to love people more than things, greater optimism and happiness, and the certainty that they are part of something larger than themselves. Many years from now, they will remember you with gratitude.

I have written this book in user-friendly language. The chapters are comprised of brief sections, each describing a key, beneficial parental habit. I believe that in today's time-challenged, information-saturated culture, brevity is a kindness that helps us to gain and retain understanding. Each section concludes with a list of key points as an additional memory aid. I address *your* habits rather than your child's for two important reasons. First, the only behaviors we have some degree of control over are our own. Second, our habits are the most important model for those of our child.

You may find yourself using this book in a variety of ways. *Simple Habits of Exceptional (But Not Perfect) Parents* may start out as a parenting primer that helps set the course of your lifelong parenting journey. Later, when family circumstances raise important challenges, you may open to this or that chapter for a refresher. For some readers, the book may become an always-ready coach to consult regularly—for reminders or when you simply feel like affirming the great job you're doing as a parent.

Now, an important disclaimer: While I strive to be an exceptional parent, I am, alas, only human. As my son, Erik, now 24 and working at his first post-college "real" job, can attest, I do my best to be an exceptional parent and I am also far from perfect. The years have taught me to value humility as inspiration for lifelong learning. This book shares what I have learned as well as what I aspire to achieve.

I wrote this book after several of my therapy clients suggested that I share the advice I gave them with a wider audience. I offer the pages that follow hoping that they will help you practice

Ken Dolan-Del Vecchio

these simple habits, which in turn, will help your child live a joyful, healthy, and successful life. As one parent to another, give your child this gift—you, an exceptional parent. Twenty years from now, you'll still be glad you did.

Enter your name here: _____

Enter today's date here: _____

Chapter 1
Habits of Heart and Mind

In the end, only kindness matters.
—Jewel Kilcher, singer-songwriter

Ken Dolan-Del Vecchio

Heart and mind: Where everything we set out to do begins. The internal chatter of our thoughts and the intensity of our heart-felt feelings shape one another and, together, they shape our behavior. Because we generally have more control over what we think than how we feel, acknowledging, evaluating, and then changing some of our thoughts can be a key first step to changing our behavior. The most research-validated approach to psychotherapy, cognitive behavioral therapy, is based upon this principle—a principle we can use in our lives, every day.

This chapter will help you examine your thoughts and feelings about crucial aspects of parenting and, where helpful, assist you in changing your behavior. Specifically, the chapter will explore the power we hold as parents and help you use your power in ways that are always loving. It will help you cherish your child's individuality, be the best possible role model for them, and show them how to make sense of the many strange challenges we face in this day and age.

Here's a personal example of how examining my thoughts has helped me to change my behavior. While I want to consistently show love, I have also caught myself letting my attention drift, impatiently, when Erik needed a listening ear. I remember walking through a shopping mall one day when Erik was four years old or so. We strolled along, me holding his hand and drifting into my thoughts about all that we needed to get done that day. My reverie was interrupted by "Dad ...Dad, you're not even listening to me!"

Looking inward and talking things over with people I trust have helped me recognize some of the thoughts behind this behavior. I've looked at how my upbringing as a man combined with my parents' great emphasis on busyness and accomplishment taught me to value *getting things done* over *listening carefully to what another person has to say*. While *getting things done* within my profession requires careful listening, when I am away from work and back in the cocoon of family relationships I may too readily default to earlier, ingrained habits.

Wanting to change this behavior, I have worked to change the beliefs and values behind it by emphasizing this thought: *My first priority is caring for my child and that includes listening carefully to what he has to say.* Keeping this resolution close to the front of my mind has helped me stay more emotionally present with Erik, which in turn, has brought more joy into my life and, I hope, into his as well.

Most of us strive to become better parents. Let's face it, though, changing our behavior ranks high among life's great challenges. As we move ahead, I'll share more of my own stories and suggestions. My most important recommendations: Treat yourself gently as you work toward change and never fear asking others for help. Kind actions toward ourselves bring energy, solace, and much-needed guidance. They also help us to accept that we, like our children, will always be works-in-progress.

The Power of Love

One aspect of the relationship every parent creates with his or her child is so basic and ever-present that we tend not to pay it any attention. Inattention, however, can invite unfortunate consequences. I'm talking about the way we use power. Broadly speaking, we have two options. The first is to use power to dominate and control—to exercise *power over* another human being. This way of using power shows up so consistently that we may find it hard to imagine any other possibility. Supervisors in many of our workplaces demonstrate *power over*, commanding and controlling those who report to them.

Fortunately, we have another option—an exceptional choice that brings exceptional value. This second option sees power not as the opportunity to dominate and control but rather to care for others and bring about good things for everybody involved. Often called *power with*, this way of using power is the essence of love, for the love we feel for others becomes evident to them through our actions. Riane Eisler's book *The Chalice and the Blade,* which I first read many years ago, is where I learned of these two visions

3

of power and they have served as an invaluable tool ever since. As parents, we use *power with* when we consistently care for, respect, include and value our child. As a result, our daughter or son will likely gain self-respect, self-esteem, and happiness—and he or she will feel loved. Exceptional parents know this and act accordingly.

They key message here: Recognize the power you hold as a parent and always use your power as love. The words *recognize* and *always* deserve special emphasis in that sentence. For while we have more brainpower, experience and judgment than our children, and despite our obvious differences in physical size and strength, we often get confused about who holds the balance of power, behave inconsistently, and use our advantages in unloving ways. In doing so, we risk handing our children a host of avoidable difficulties.

Before saying more about why this happens and how to stick with the habit of using power as love rather than as domination, let's take a closer look at power itself. Let's examine what it is, how we get it, why it's important and why we sometimes use it in ways that do not benefit our children.

Power is the ability to shape many important aspects of our lives, including the ease with which we acquire essentials such as food, water, safety, and shelter. The amount of power we have also shapes the ways that we interact with other people, the world of work and the natural world. The more power we hold, the more control we have over the way we spend our time and energy. The less power we hold, the more our time and energy will likely be devoted to activities directed by other people.

Each of us begins life as a powerless infant. From that point on, we gain power through gifts of nature and from the people who care for us. Many of these power-enhancing gifts develop over the course of years, including our size, physical strength, and our ever-improving ability to communicate, exercise self-control, and develop other social skills.

In our culture and many others, we draw a great deal of our power from the amount of money we accumulate and the extent to which we enjoy positive connections with people who have even more than we do. A young man who lived in my college dorm boasted that his parents had paid a lot of money for his exclusive prep-school education. He gloated about how this investment paid off not so much because of the school's superb course of studies but, rather, because he befriended a scion of one of the U.S.'s most wealthy and powerful political families and the sons of two corporate chief executive officers. He expected these friendships to help him land a prestigious job after graduating from college.

We also gain power through education and training that lead to professional credentials and occupational skills. Many of us also accumulate power through life experiences that teach us how the world works—what some people call "street smarts."

Every relationship is shaped by the relative power of those involved. My previous book, *Making Love, Playing Power: Men, Women, and the Rewards of Intimate Justice,* explored this topic in depth. Most important for our purpose here: The way the more powerful person in an important long-term relationship uses their power shapes the experiences and, ultimately, the character of the person who has less power. This is never truer than in our relationships with our children.

When we live this key message—*always recognize the power you hold and use it as love*—our children feel safe and secure in our presence. They will likely gain confidence, try new experiences with a spirit of adventure, and learn mutual trust and respect. The importance of how we parents use power cannot be overstated.

Learning to use parental power in such a constructive way can be challenging, however. Some of us don't fully realize the degree of power we have over our child's development, and we can't use our power effectively if we don't know that we have it in the first place. Others of us recognize our power but, perhaps because we feel overwhelmed by stress or because we're following what we saw our own parents do, sometimes use our power in negative ways.

Many factors contribute to the difficulties we face. As I mentioned at the outset of this discussion, we live in a world flush with examples of power being used to possess, control and dominate. The daily news tells of political leaders, military officers and titans of the business world commanding those who answer to them. Closer to home and as I mentioned earlier, most of us face *power over* every day at work. Our bosses tell us what to do and, in some cases, even when and how to do it.

Finding ourselves mostly on the downside of this *power over* world, many of us feel relatively powerless and may not see that, when it comes to our children at least, we actually hold a great deal of power. Some parents may not recognize that any alternative to *power over* exists. Other fathers and mothers may simply feel too exhausted by stress to parent their child with consistency.

The Powerless Parent

For these and other reasons, we sometimes do not exercise parental authority much at all. When this happens, we risk setting our children adrift in the world with little supervision, something all children badly need. When we don't exercise parental power, our child may find him or herself by default in a position of *power over* their parent. I can almost see you cringe while reading those words, and rightly so, for we've all seen the resulting dramas and most of us have at one time or another played the role of parental co-star: A child of four or five years old wails at deafening volume and flails her little arms and legs while strapped into a hair-cutter or dentist's chair, her exasperated parent begging for quiet. Largely disregarded, mom or dad surrenders into passive hope that the emotional storm will pass quickly. They coo and stroke their child's hair or bounce a toy in front of her red, tear-soaked face.

Perhaps you're more familiar with the "But I want it!" scene that plays out every day in retail stores across the land. When Erik was a preschooler, I was the parent in this scene more times than I want to recall. While details vary, the plot always goes more or less like this: A child and his parent on a run to the grocery, pharmacy or department store reach a standoff. The little boy or girl has grasped an item, perhaps a plastic super-hero figurine or piece of candy, and insists upon owning it. The close-to-surrender parent argues feebly against the purchase, but to no avail, for the little heart is resolute.

A variation on theme finds the parent filling an even more dubious role. Once while I was visiting relatives, the couple's 5-year-old son, who was sequestered in his upstairs bedroom, flew into a rage. He yelled and threw things, some of which, judging by the impact tremors, carried a good bit of weight. Drawing no attention, he began leaping up and down at the top of the staircase, all the while shrieking at the top of his lungs. At the peak of this performance he hurled down the stairs what I later learned was one of his favorite toys, a well-worn stuffed dog. The boy's father rose from the table, where he'd been sitting alongside me, stomped to the foot of stairs and stooped to grab the stuffed animal. He gripped the dog's oversized head and front legs in one hand, its rear legs and tail in the other, raised the toy to chest height and—glaring at his son—ripped the stuffed animal apart. The boy's screams reached ear-splitting volume. This father's behavior, while perhaps understandable, made the situation worse rather than better.

Every child behaves in ways that call for guidance. That's what it means to be a child. When we have let go of our parental power we tend to react with exasperation, confusion, surrender, anger or some combination thereof, none of which helps. Similar behavior often comes when we take a loose approach to parental authority not because we feel powerless, but because we don't want to dominate our children. In both cases, we are not recognizing and consistently exercising our power as love. Instead, in these circumstances, we abandon our parental authority and, as a result, offer no constructive response to the normal, immaturely expressed fears, desires, frustrations, and distress of our children. We respond like hostages, court jesters, or, in the final example above, like another child besting the tantrum of their age-mate with a bigger tantrum of our own.

Ken Dolan-Del Vecchio

The Perils of *Power Over*

At the other end of the *power over* spectrum, we parents may at times wholeheartedly embrace our power to dominate. Taking this to the extreme, we may impose an agenda on our child that includes activities, goals and expectations of achievement chosen exclusively by us. We may schedule soccer, baseball, scouting, dance and acting classes, whether or not our son or daughter has shown the slightest interest in these activities. We may even assume the right to direct our child's tastes in all things: music, friends, pastimes, and occupations.

While a freshman in college, I was surprised to meet many fellow students whose parents expected them to become a physician, engineer, lawyer or psychologist. *Expected* isn't quite a strong enough word, actually. *Assigned* better captures the spirit.

Many of these 18-year-olds dutifully followed through with their prescribed curriculums, all the while lamenting their disagreement with the choice that had been made for them. Now, many decades later, I have met such individuals who abandoned their parent-prescribed profession in midlife, having gained the self-knowledge and mustered the courage and self-esteem necessary to claim a life of their own choosing.

Sometimes, parents assert *power over* because of fear. We worry so much about safety and doubt so thoroughly our child's ability to succeed that we try to run our son or daughter's life. Several years back I saw a couple in therapy who rented an apartment near the university their daughter attended, which was several hours away from the family's home in New Jersey. Their daughter lived in a dorm. The apartment was for her parents' use. They had decided to take turns living there so they could oversee her studies and other activities. While based on the best of intentions, such attempts at control almost always make a child feel unsafe and incompetent, exactly what we seek to prevent.

Some parents—most of us, I'd wager—see a bit of ourselves in at least a few of the descriptions above. I know I do. I believe we sometimes falter in constructively exercising our power because, for most of us, asserting power feels unpleasant and unloving because our most obvious model remains *power over*. Bright new possibilities appear, however, when we change the definition.

Exploring *Power With*

When we shift to *power with,* the goal becomes creating good experiences for all involved. While mainstream culture continues to glorify the power of domination, examples of *power with* can be found. We see it when an orchestra conductor guides her musician colleagues through a soaring performance. We see this kind of power when studying how the human brain coordinates heart rate, breathing and other bodily functions in accordance with whether we're lying down, walking, or running and when we observe a police officer deftly directing the flow of traffic at a major intersection.

Embracing *power with*, the exceptional parent claims the awesome responsibility to facilitate their child's growth and development. *Power with* never dominates but instead expects a child to behave childishly and prepares in advance to offer guidance, limits, role-modeling, praise, and constructive consequences as fits the situation and the child's needs. When we demonstrate *power with* we help our child coordinate her or his efforts to reach achievements *our child* values. Responsibility, thoughtfulness, mutual respect and assertiveness on behalf of one's child, not oneself, lie at its core.

It's important to note that *power with* can require more time for thinking and planning than *power over*. When pressed for time—and, therefore, perhaps impatient—we may too readily default into command and control mode. We may feel a need to march our child from one errand to the next on a get-it-all-done Saturday afternoon. Our intense work schedule, other pressing responsibilities and experience with our own parents may reinforce our belief that our child should accompany us without complaint. After all, a lifetime of experience assures us that haircuts, dentist appointments and visits to the grocery store offer nothing to fear or get riled about. We assume our child feels the same way. This is *power over*—expecting another person to do it *my* way. Practicing *power with* requires a different approach.

Let's revisit some of the previous examples and see how they'd be handled differently by a parent employing *power with,* the power of love. The first step: getting in tune the other person's perspective. In other words, a key to *power with* is empathy. Putting themselves in their little one's booties, the exceptional parent sees that new experiences can frighten children, particularly a child whose temperament leans toward shyness or timidity. This parent realizes that a first haircut or dental appointment may scare their child. Consequently, they bring their little one to the hair stylist and dentist when they, the parent, have their own appointments. The child sits on their mom or dad's lap while the stylist works his or her magic. The exceptional parent engages their child in conversation about the fun of getting a haircut and wonders aloud about the fun their child will have with their own very first haircut adventure. Similarly, the exceptional parent brings their child along for a dental visit, explaining beforehand what to expect and describing how important it is to sit quietly while the dental technician and dentist do their work. In this case, the parent brings along another adult who can sit with their child while Mom or Dad occupies the dentist's chair.

The exceptional parent uses *power with,* the power of love, to turn what may have become a frightening and exasperating experience into an opportunity for learning, exploration and maturation. Remember, *power with* expects children to behave immaturely and provides experience, knowledge and role-modeling to build age-appropriate understanding and growth. Planning and delivering preparatory learning experiences distinguish this way of using power.

Before departing on a trip to the grocery store, the exceptional parent asks their child which toy they'd like to bring along. Before exiting the car, this exceptional parent says to their little one, "Ok, don't forget to bring your toy! And while we're at the store, don't be surprised if some other toys or candies catch your eye. Remember, we're only here to buy food for dinner and nothing else this trip. So, you can look, but not touch." I learned to use this approach with Erik and it worked!

When planning for a relative's visit, the exceptional parent considers the stress this can cause a child, who may temporarily lose his or her ability to get as much attention from adults. Planning includes brainstorming ways to include the child. Anticipating the child's normal desire for center stage moments (and who doesn't want to be the center of attention sometimes?) the parent considers how this wish can be gratified by including and celebrating the child as an important member of the family.

When a child throws a tantrum, *power with* does not try to overpower her or him with an even more extreme display of unpleasant behavior, such as shouting even louder than the child or breaking something the child values. Instead, the child's parent speaks in a quiet voice that invites the child to calm down. If necessary, the parent embraces the child in a way that quiets but does not hurt them, holding them still until their body relaxes. If the tantrum occurs in a public place—a store or restaurant—the parent also removes the child from the premises so that his or her behavior doesn't bother other people. Once the child has stilled for several seconds, the parent praises them for calming down, then talks with them about what just happened. The parent may assign reasonable consequences:

- "I want you to stay here in your room and take five minutes to calm down completely. Then I'll come back and we'll decide what the two of us will do together."
- "You and I are going home now so we can talk about how I can help you stay calm when we're at a store or restaurant. I

want you to be able to come with me and not have to stay at home next time."

For teenagers, *power with* delivers authoritative guidance and consequences that suit the child's more advanced stage of development:

- "The house rule is lights out and no electronic communication after 10 p.m. on weeknights. You need to leave your phone and laptop on the kitchen table." If the child breaks this rule, the parent may take away computer and phone privileges for a brief period as a consequence.
- A child who uses her parent's car and comes home later than agreed upon may be told that the car will be temporarily unavailable to her if she does this again. If the teen comes home late a second time, it is reasonable for a parent to remove her access to the car for two weeks.

As a child grows, *power with* recognizes the difference between *exploring* and *assigning* new activities. *Power with* asks the child if he or she would like to try dance, violin, soccer, or baseball and then lets them explore their interests in order to learn more about themselves. In those cases in which a child shows *no* interest in *any* activities, a parent may decide that some degree of gentle insistence makes sense. Signing up for one or more guitar lessons where they and their child can learn together or for a beginner's lesson of some other sort may inspire the child's personal exploration.

When a child shows no interest in activities that we love, we may naturally feel disappointed. The exceptional parent manages this feeling with care. He or she may wisely choose to talk through their disappointment with other adults, but they spare their son or daughter. A child stands to gain nothing but undeserved guilt and a negative jolt to their self-esteem by learning they have disappointed their parent in such a fashion.

Later, we'll examine more closely how *power with* shapes such necessary parental actions as limit-setting and delivering reasonable consequences so children can learn self-monitoring, self-soothing and social skills. As mentioned previously, the use of power informs everything else we do as parents.

I find the power of love to be in increasingly short supply. The power of domination, on the other hand, continues to make headlines on a daily basis. As I mentioned at the beginning of this conversation, however, the power of love, the exceptional choice, delivers exceptional benefits. When we use our power as love, we care for our children, supporting their health and fulfillment and helping them develop into their unique potential. Those who apply power in this fashion help others experience fairness, shared success and benefits of many kinds. In fact, the qualities most of us deeply value—self-esteem, self-knowledge, assertiveness, feelings of competence, the ability to critically evaluate events and the willingness to trust our own judgment—begin with the power of love. Tyrants wield *power over*; statespersons, great leaders and exceptional parents, *power with,* the power of love.

Key Points

1. There are essentially two ways of understanding and using power: domination (*power over*) and love (*power with*).

2. Most of us sometimes default to *power over,* the kind of power glorified in our culture, particularly when we feel tired, preoccupied or overwhelmed.

3. Exceptional parents remain aware of the power they hold and strive to use their power as love.

4. Using our power in a consistently loving fashion calls for understanding our child's stage of development, planning ahead and creating opportunities that help our child learn from new experiences (haircuts, dentist visits, being cared for by a sitter, for example).

Ken Dolan-Del Vecchio

Who Owns This Life?

After our son Erik was born, his mom Lynn and I mused, as parents do, about who our tiny new person would become. Would he become a man of great renown, a researcher who discovers the cure for cancer, a leader who helps humanity forge lasting world peace, or perhaps the scientist whose work saves life on Earth from spiraling environmental crises? In less grandiose moments, we'd wonder whether he'd become a lawyer or family therapist or physician or veterinarian or businessman. Maybe he'd work as a plumber or carpenter or auto repair technician; or in sales, selling financial services or solar installations, or computer technology. We wondered about his temperament. Will he be unrelentingly opinionated or someone who'll always listen with care and negotiate a reasonable compromise, or somewhere in between? Will he be a "just the facts" kind of guy or intuitive and artistic? The future of our little boy lay before us, open to possibility.

Through these conversations about great unknowns, Lynn and I realized that we did know something important: Whoever Erik would become would be revealed to us by Erik, for this new life did not belong to us, nor our extended family or a particular community of faith or the United States government or any other entity or person. Erik's life belonged entirely to Erik.

While Lynn and I made our share of parenting mistakes over the years, I will always be grateful that we got this right. In my family therapy practice, in conversations with friends, family and colleagues, and on the sidelines of soccer and baseball fields while Erik and his friends played, I have encountered many parents who behave as though their child's unfolding life offers the last best hope for achieving their own dreams. Sitting in the bleachers at one of my son's baseball games when he was eight years old I overheard one dad say to another, "I think my kid can go all the way to the majors if he gives it everything he has, and I'll help in any way possible!" Don't let this recipe for pain happen to you.

The key message here: Make a habit of appreciating your child's uniqueness. You can help them fulfill their own special potential, most importantly, their potential for happiness.

My friend Jerry, a managing director in a financial services firm, and his wife Allison, an attorney, practice this habit with their two children, Marybeth and Justin. Marybeth, now 17 and a junior in high school, recently started driving and has begun to narrow the choices of colleges to which she'll apply. Everyone in the family supports Marybeth's exploration, looking forward with excitement to the next stage of her young life. She and her parents have discussed a variety of vocational options that may suit her and at present she's focused on veterinary medicine. "I'll probably start off at college as a pre-vet student and see how that fits me," Marybeth says.

In years past, Jerry and Allison supported Marybeth's interests in swimming. Concerned for her safety and also wanting to allow her to explore, when Marybeth expressed an interest in scuba diving, Jerry joined her in taking lessons. He came to love the sport even more than she does.

At 13, Justin, an eighth-grader, follows a path different from many of his peers. He's an avid fan of several fantasy websites, closely following the exploits of the larger-than-life heroes and heroines found there. He loves attending "fantasy fan conferences," many of whose attendees dress as characters from their favorite stories. So far, Jerry and Allison have accompanied their son to two fantasy conferences. While his parents don't share Justin's interest in the genre, they love the creativity Justin brings to the costumes he makes and the joy this hobby brings him.

Justin spends most of his free time with friends who are girls. For as long as they can remember, Justin's parents have also noted his interest in wearing his sister's clothes. Since age three, Justin has wondered aloud about whether he should have been born a girl rather than a boy. Recently, he has begun saying, "I'm probably transgender."

As you may imagine, Jerry and Allison have struggled with how best to respond. From the beginning, they've faced worries and feelings of loss, for it can be heart-wrenching indeed to have your hopes for your child's future dissolve into fears for their safety as you consider the bias and stigma directed toward people who are different in this way.

After Justin said "I should probably have been a girl" for the third or fourth time, Jerry and Allison sought help from a therapist with expertise in gender identity. Their consultations have continued since then, with Justin and Marybeth sometimes included, and Justin meeting alone with the family's therapist at times also.

Allison and Jerry have made a point of discussing their son's difference with his day care center professionals and, later, professionals at Justin's schools. Fortunately, they live in a town where the schools back up their inclusion policies with action. On the few occasions in which Justin has faced teasing by boys and girls about his lack of interest in baseball, basketball, and football, and about his friendships with girls, school personnel have intervened directly with these children and their parents in ways that ended this behavior.

Jerry and Allison have talked with Justin since his pre-school years about the negativity that people who appear different too often encounter from others. They have encouraged him to experiment only at home with his preferred mix of boys' and girls' clothing, a style of dress that would almost certainly draw the attention of bullies. They also enrolled Justin in Tae Kwon Do classes when he was four and he continues to excel at this sport. He has recently taken up weight training as a means to further develop his strength, confidence and overall health.

Justin currently attends a program for transgender youth recommended by the family's therapist and pediatrician. He plans to join the Gay, Lesbian, Bisexual, Transgender, and Straight Alliance at the high school he'll attend next year. Unlike some gender non-conforming children, Jerry and his parents, after consulting with the family's pediatrician, have decided not to start Justin on the hormone therapy that would block the bodily changes that come with puberty. Justin has decided that he wants to gain the muscularity and body proportions that come with being male while he continues what he calls his "adventure in gender."

Allison and Jerry plan to continue their family's consultations with helping professionals so they can all flourish in a world where stigma, bullying and worse still threaten the health and safety of people like Justin. While supporting Justin's exploration, Jerry and Allison have made every effort to help Marybeth understand her sibling's emerging gender identity as well. These efforts have taken hold, with Marybeth recently telling Justin, "It's cool to be the only one I know who has a gender non-conforming sibling."

While many of our child's interests and attributes that differ from our own will enrich their lives and perhaps ours as well, some may warrant special concern. If your child shows unrelenting interest in hurting other children or animals, remains listless and negative much of the time, seems drawn to hate groups, or is chronically anxious, these patterns deserve special attention. It makes sense to consult with your child's guidance counselor or a family therapist.

When Allison, Jerry, and other exceptional parents meet their newborn child for the very first time, they, like the rest of us parents, undoubtedly marvel at the family resemblances in the face that gazes back at them. Like Lynn and me, they likely wonder aloud about who their family's new addition will become in this world. All of this imagining fades, however, as they get to know their baby as a real human being, an individual with interests and talents all their own. Exceptional parents appreciate each characteristic of their new family member, and they do what they can to help him or her explore what the world has to offer. The following exercises can help you cultivate support for your child's unique gifts:

- Observe and name ways that your child's aptitudes, interests and temperament both resemble and differ from your own, his or her other parent and extended family members. For example, you and your daughter may share a love of horses. At the same time, she may love being the center of attention while you savor your alone time.

- Discuss with another adult whom you trust how the ways that you and your child seem both similar and different enrich both of your lives. For example, my politically conservative friends, Pat and Geri, told me that their second child, Kevin, now 14, argues for the election of a socialist presidential candidate. Geri says, "He makes some good points and Pat and I have actually moved a little in Kevin's direction, while he seems to have moved a bit in ours."

- Make a point of learning more about some of your child's interests that are unfamiliar to you. My son and his girlfriend recently moved to Germany, a place I'd never been. I'm learning a few German words and had a great time visiting them last month.

- Practice naming as many of your child's character traits as you can. Many descriptions fit our son when he was little, including smiley, interested in other people, a lover of cats, dogs, and horses, deep sleeper, tentative but curious in new situations, friendly, trusting, musical, energetic, flexible, adaptable, great about trying new food and easily amused. He could also be cranky and stubborn. (On the whole, we were very lucky: He was an especially easy baby.)

- Notice and name your child's likes and dislikes. Help them identify and put these into words also. "You really love your guitar lessons but you're not so interested in the classic rock that your mom and I grew up listening to."

- Compliment yourself and your co-parent, if you have one, for supporting your child's pursuits that lie beyond your own personal interests and talents. I know divorced parents who each have taken their son and his friends to theme parks, paint ball arenas, carnivals, zip-line adventures, and concerts by teen-sensation rock bands. They make a point of thanking one another for taking their son to places that neither of them have much interest in visiting.

- Write a sentence of two affirming your belief in your child's right to his or her own life, which may differ significantly from your own when it comes to interests, spirituality, sexual orientation, gender identity, educational path, occupational interest, where they choose to settle in the world geographically, and the people with whom they choose to associate.
- Closely examine anything that you want very badly for your child to help you decide whether what you want may actually be misplaced and more accurately belong to you. For example, if you want your one-year-old to grow up to play the market like Warren Buffet or sing like Beyonce, it's important to recognize that this desire belongs to you and you alone. Your child may have entirely different aspirations.

Practicing these exercises will sharpen your ability to celebrate the unique individual with whom your family has been blessed. You'll learn, perhaps paradoxically, that the more we parents recognize and value how our child differs from us, the closer we feel to them (and they to us).

Key Points:
1. Make a habit of appreciating your child's uniqueness.
2. It's wonderful to envision great success for your child, but make sure the details of your vision reflect your child's unique talents and dreams rather than dreams of your own that you assign to them.
3. It can help to make a habit of noticing, naming and valuing both the similarities and differences between you and your child.
4. Valuing the differences between you and your child will likely bring you closer to each other.

Ken Dolan-Del Vecchio

Who's Watching Whom?

I remember the feeling. I'd be in the middle of a grocery shopping expedition and suddenly feel somebody watching me. Looking around and then slightly downward, my eyes would meet those of my one-year-old son, his butt nested in the crook of my elbow and eyes fixed on my face. His face would erupt into a smile. I'd smile in return and say, "Hi, Erik! What are you looking at?" He'd giggle.

How many times in the rush to get things done did I briefly lose sight of the fact that he was with me, as close as one person can get to another, and watching my every move? He took in the way I spoke to the grocery store cashier, the things I muttered under my breath while rushing through the aisles, the grumbling about crowds, prices, and other talk-to-myself gripes meant for my ears alone. Erik paid attention to it all, *everything I said and did*. Your child is no different.

Children learn much about how to be in the world through observation, and they focus most steadily on their parents. The key message here: Your child is always watching you as a key role model—*always*!

While I wrote *watching,* the truth goes deeper than that. My experience as a therapist is that children absorb far more than their parents' words and behavior. They also pay attention to our attitudes, moods, belief systems and perspectives in ways that shape their own. So much about the way we make sense of the world and interact with it with it rubs off on them, and this aspect of parenting never goes away. My father was skeptical about everything and everyone. For better or worse, his perspective has colored my own, making it difficult for me to trust. I'll say more about this later.

Our influence over our children presents a lifelong challenge to those of us who strive to be exceptional parents. We recognize that our own lives—until the moment we leave this world—will have a formative impact upon the lives of our children.

You may be scratching your head at this point, noting the puzzle this message poses when compared to that of the previous discussion, in which I encouraged parents to support the individuality of their child rather than impose their own dreams. "How can I help my child develop their unique qualities," you may wonder, "when fate commands him or her to follow my lead in so many ways?"

The answer can be found within the question. For while children undoubtedly absorb aspects of our style—our tendency toward optimism or pessimism, our ability to meet stress and change with resilience, whether our pace of living is hurried or relaxed, our openness to the new and different—our own traits are by no means the only influence we have on our children. The more consistently we support our child's unique talents, character strengths and perspectives, the more likely our child will grow fully into these particular strengths, adopting aspects of our own style to fuel their own unique potential.

The Dance of Development: How Parents Matter

For example, when exceptional parents make a habit of saving some of the money they earn, live within their means, and invest more in enriching experiences than material possessions, their children may well absorb these habits. The enriching experiences that each child chooses to purchase, however, may vary considerably according to their unique interests and aptitudes. One sibling may favor ski trips, another sibling, evenings at the opera, and a third, Habitat for Humanity missions to places devastated by natural disaster.

When exceptional parents live lives of passionate commitment to the things that matter most to them, their children are more likely to absorb the belief that life offers the opportunity for energetic commitment to one's values. The particular details of what matters most to the children of such parents may vary, but the overall vision for what life is all about may get absorbed and carried forward. Thus, one child of such parents may devote themselves to providing services for the homeless, another may study medicine, and the third may work to promote clean energy, each deriving great satisfaction from lives with very different guiding passions.

When Role Modeling Goes Wrong

Of course, not everything our children see us do benefits them. At some point in our lives, most of us behave regrettably. My grandfather, Pasquale Del Vecchio, was a generally loving, thoughtful and intelligent man. When I think of him now, I see a balding man in his early seventies nested in his easy chair, which was tucked somewhat oddly into a kitchen corner. There he'd sit, smoking his pipe and reading a novel by Mario Puzo or a work of political journalism by one investigative reporter or another.

I also recall a second image. Pasquale loved to garden. He raised vegetables on a half-acre section of his property and flower beds decorated the remainder of his two-acre lot. His garden handiwork, which included breeding his own varieties of tulips and other perennials, brought him enormous satisfaction.

One side of his property touched the concrete sidewalk bordering a tiny residential street (ironically named Majestic Avenue). Here, Pasquale grew a dense privet hedge that he kept perfectly trimmed at a height of seven feet. There came a time when boisterous children walking to and from school took to throwing one another into the hedge. This continued even after my grandfather sternly warned them (and their parents) against damaging his prized greenery.

Pasquale moved on to Plan B. He drove two cedar posts into the earth, one post hidden inside the hedge at either end. Next, he strung a spiraling length of barbed wire between the posts, ensuring that the coils remained concealed inside the foliage. At the completion of his project the hedge's outer appearance remained unchanged but a dangerous surprise awaited any who might disturb it. Pasquale told the adults in the neighborhood what he'd done, advising them to warn their children. As far as I remember, his hedge was never troubled again.

Pasquale's eldest son, my father, Joe, carried this pattern forward. Much later, our family lived in a housing development plagued by teenaged vandals whose favorite sports seemed to be smashing mailboxes, throwing eggs at houses and parked cars, and driving over the edges of lawns. No neighborhood Halloween jack-o-lantern was safe. At some point, Dad couldn't take it anymore. When I was seven years old, after we kids carved our Halloween pumpkins we watched as my dad drove a few small nails in backwards, placing them where they'd most likely pierce the palms of any grasping neighborhood hoodlums. Our pumpkins, like all the others on the block, got smashed anyway.

My father responded similarly when, several Friday evenings in a row, a corner of our yard was scarred by tire tracks. At dusk the following Friday, Dad placed wooden planks, each impaled by many upturned nails, across that section of lawn. We knew these traps had achieved Dad's goal when, in the small hours of the morning, silence gave way to the growls of engines revving followed by the shouts and curses of young men.

I absorbed all of this vindictiveness, plus my dad's regular warning that we should always suspect that acts of kindness may conceal "an ulterior motive." As you may imagine, I have needed to do a lot of work on letting go of my father's (and grandfather's) legacy of suspicion and revenge. This came into play most recently after I gave a $700 downpayment check to a paving contractor who promised to work on my driveway the following day. He immediately cashed the check but didn't show up the following morning. After four weeks, during which I texted and phoned him, filed a complaint with the better business bureau, and—having learned that he had done this to many other customers—showed him a "scam alert" flyer that I planned to post at the libraries, post offices, and other public places in our small town, he stopped by and handed me $700 in cash.

During those four weeks, I also fantasized about violent retribution, sometimes feeling so enraged that I couldn't sleep. I became preoccupied with thoughts about slashing the contractor's tires and bashing the windows on his truck and at his place of business. There were moments when I even felt the impulse to move beyond fantasy and into action. Thankfully, I talked this all over with my husband and close friends, and they helped me put the situation in perspective. They also helped me recognize my rage and violent impulses as part of my family legacy that I can do without.

I could share many other stories about my father and grandfather, most of them far more positive. I chose to share these as cautionary tales that illustrate the ripple effect of our behavior into the minds and souls of our children. Exceptional parents keep this reality in mind. They know that our children are always watching, listening and learning from us.

Key points
1. Keep in mind that children watch their parents as their first and most important role models.
2. Remember that how you actually live will always be more meaningful to your child than what you advise.
3. A sincere apology followed by a change in behavior, something we'll discuss in detail later on, can limit the harm we cause by behaving regrettably in the presence of our child.

Believe in Yourself and Others
Monica McGoldrick, a friend and one of my family therapy mentors, has said many times, "Life is long and there are many paths to success." What if all of us parents could keep Monica's sentiment in our minds and hearts? Not always an easy task, to be sure. In fact, how many times have you heard a parent say something like this about their child: "He's got so much potential, but he seems hell-bent on wasting it!" I've also heard parents say these kinds of things directly to their children. When they do, you can bet that

their underlying concern—wanting their child to succeed—gets obscured by their words and tone. Their words assault the child's belief in their own competence, deepening any shame she or he already feels. The key message here: Exceptional parents believe in themselves and their children. They know there are many paths to joy, health and success, and they support their child's choices.

I recently consulted with a couple whose nineteen-year-old son, Gabe, faced a challenging time adjusting to college life. Gabe had traveled from his home in New York City to attend a Midwestern university. His first time away from home for an extended period, the young man had difficulty keeping up with his coursework and making friends.

Gabe's parents, Ellen and Michael, only learned of their son's struggles when he mentioned during the Thanksgiving holiday that he might fail two of his classes if he didn't soon hand in overdue writing assignments. Gabe felt reasonably certain that he'd get the work done and end the semester with a B average. He also mentioned that he was considering withdrawing from college and seeking full-time employment because, in his words, "I'm not really sure what I want out of college." Gabe reasoned that a year or two in the job market might help him gain clarity, allowing him to return to college when he felt ready to focus on a course of study that truly interested him.

Ellen and Michael took Gabe's words as evidence of mental instability. They called me for an appointment and also began looking for a psychiatrist, for they were sure the young man needed medication in addition to talk therapy.

"You're talking about throwing your life away," Michael told Gabe. "And we're not going to just stand by and let that happen!"

The couple and I began exploring their fears. Gabe was not interested in participating so I never got to meet him firsthand. The long-held story Ellen and Michael had developed about their son told of a "brilliant but unfocused" child who, without their supervision, would likely ruin his life through foolish decision-making. It fell to Michael and Ellen, as their story went, to safeguard Gabe's dazzling future by rescuing him from the self-sabotage that would inevitably occur if he were left to his own choices. They held this view despite the fact that twice during Gabe's school years, at their request, he been evaluated for learning and other behavioral health difficulties, with each assessment finding no problems.

Interestingly, while Ellen and Michael felt sure Gabe would come to ruin without their constant oversight, they also felt certain of their son's potential for greatness. If they did their job properly, they believed, Gabe would leave his foolishness behind one day and embark upon an extraordinarily successful adult life.

I wondered aloud how they would recognize the moment when this remarkable transformation arrived.

I asked, "How will Gabe make his transition to competence without ever experiencing the consequences of his unfortunate decisions and the opportunities for learning these afford?" and, "What do you think it feels like to grow up with the kind of parental attention you've been giving Gabe?"

Somewhat offended, Ellen said, "We love our son dearly and just want to spare him avoidable pitfalls."

Michael nodded his agreement.

I pressed: "What do you think the person on the receiving end would call what you've been describing?"

Eventually, we got to words like *micromanagement, control, invalidation, over-protectiveness, hovering and shaming.*

I shared with the couple the vision I saw in my mind's eye when I considered their concern for Gabe: I saw them imagining a glowing moment far in the future, a time when their child would be a man of great accomplishments. Between the present and that time, however, they saw him walking a very narrow strip of level land atop an unfathomably steep mountain range. One false move and he would topple into the abyss. Their job: to make sure that false move never happened.

I challenged them to work with me toward imagining a different story. Together, we crafted it. In this story, the light came not from a pinpoint in the distance but from directly overhead, the midday sun illuminating a broad landscape. Gabe stood on solid ground that stretched as far as the eye could see. To the north, the terrain lay flat, blooming with meadows of purple and yellow. To the east, woodland grew just a few paces ahead, trees concealing what lay beyond. Westward saw a rocky outcrop at the edge of a swiftly flowing stream, beyond which gentle hills and valleys rolled. Finally, to the south stood a great mountain range, its snowcapped summits shining silver in the distance.

In this vision, from where the young man stood he might choose to move in any direction. With each choice he would walk on solid ground. Each would traverse landscapes offering different kinds of beauty, challenge and opportunities for learning. Different choices led to different destinations, each of which held the potential for joy, health and success. In this new vision, a variety of paths, none yet chosen, promised adventure more than danger, hope more than the specter of catastrophe.

Many times we distrust the decisions and judgment our children make because we distrust our own. Another way to put this: It can be hard to believe in our child when we don't believe in ourselves. Sometimes our greatest fear is that our child will turn out just like us.

Many years ago I was visiting Lynnette, a friend from college, shortly after we'd both graduated. During my visit, Lynnette, one of the most competent people I know, received a job offer as a systems analyst—her first "real job" offer after college and her dream come true. She had weathered a series of interviews, learning along the way that the pool of candidates was large and well qualified, so her offer of employment counted as a great achievement. I was there when she made the announcement to her parents. "I'm thrilled," she told them. Lynnette described her new duties in some detail, sharing how she'd be interviewing various business people, mapping out their work flows, and then helping computer programmers design systems that would allow the group to automate some of their tasks, better document their work, and make their jobs easier overall.

Her father struck first. With arms crossed and face crunched into an expression of disbelief, he said, "You mean to tell me that you're qualified to do that—figure out how to make the work done in an office fit with a computer programmer's specifications?" His tone bordered on derisive. "They're going to trust you, fresh out of school, with that kind of work?"

Mom followed with, "How did you convince them to hire you? Aren't you worried about being able to pull this off?"

Like a balloon pricked by a needle, Lynnette got smaller right before my eyes. In a deflated voice, she told her parents that the job would help her further develop skills that she'd learned at college and during two summer internships. "I have no worries about my ability to succeed, and I look forward to the challenge," she said, her voice flat. With that, Lynnette left the room and gestured for me to follow.

I've come to learn that scenes such as this and those described earlier are less likely to indicate the child's actual degree of competence than the parent's belief in their own ability to navigate life. People who believe in their own competence, who approach life's challenges with a spirit of adventure and the conviction that they will be successful, tend to radiate that belief toward others. Such people see life as a mosaic of opportunities and challenges that invite adventure, learning and achievement. They react to the new and unexpected with appreciation and curiosity rather than fear and avoidance. When other people, including their children, throw them a curveball, they catch it and stay in the game, asking thoughtful questions, appreciating the unexpected possibilities raised, and never faltering in their belief in the other person.

Personally, in order to come closer to this ideal, I need to stay aware of thoughts and feelings that undermine my belief in myself and take corrective action. Sometimes that means recalling previous challenges and the knowledge and skills that helped me succeed, as when I received my most recent promotion at work and wasn't sure I could handle the new responsibilities. Thinking about my previous successes as a leader reassured me that I had what it takes to meet the challenges ahead. Reminding myself that growth comes from risk-taking helped as well.

Over the years, connecting with mentors, therapists and coaches has helped me gain skills and confidence as a parent, therapist and student of crafts that include gardening, raising livestock and writing. Reading books—such as the one you have in your hands—has also been a great source of help. I often remind myself that there is no shame in being imperfect. On the contrary, it allows life to be a never-ending adventure in learning.

It is possible to respond helpfully even when we feel insecure about some of our own life choices and doubtful about those made by our child. We can listen respectfully to what our child has to say, *validate the child's experience* and, if the situation warrants, *ask how we may be able to help.* The key word there is *ask,* because we as parents have no other way of knowing the most helpful course of action.

We simply cannot appreciate another human being's life situation with greater authority than they can personally. Nobody lives inside the mind and heart of another. Nor can we ultimately control the path our child will follow.

This reality becomes clearer as our child advances toward adulthood. With every year that passes, our degree of control over their behavior withers. We may wisely work to maintain a loving relationship, one that allows us to provide positive influence, but we lose the degree of control we had when our child was small.

Some parents must confront this truth at its starkest. Despite their consistently loving care and positive role-modeling, their child behaves in ways unhealthy or even dangerous to themselves or others. Their child may have fallen into the downward spiral of addiction or engaged in criminal activity. A parent in this circumstance may want desperately to "save their child from themselves." Unfortunately, we can't do that. We *can* set house rules (if our child lives in our home or visits regularly) and establish consequences for their violation. We can meet with professional helpers to decide how best to respond to our child's troubling behavior and also care for ourselves during this stressful time, and decide whether or not to pay for bail and a top-notch attorney. But we can't control our child's behavior.

I'd like to stress here that we may demonstrate the most exceptional parenting possible and *still* our child may face a lifetime of troubles. While parenting will always be vitally important, many other variables—genetics, peer relationships, trauma experienced outside the family, and other factors beyond parental reach—contribute to character development and behavior. While we owe it to ourselves and our child to strive for exceptional parenting, we also owe ourselves gentleness and acceptance when it comes to forces beyond our control.

Reviewing where we've traveled together through previous chapters, I can tell you that exceptional parents always strive to respond to their child in a way that's loving rather than controlling. They want to learn more about what their child thinks and feels about their current challenges, knowing that this information is more relevant than what they, the parents think and feel. They want to model calm, respect, concern and helpfulness.

Exceptional parents know that, while they may personally credit their own success to earning a particular college degree, passing a civil service exam, belonging to their community of faith, earning a certain amount of money, or reaching some other milestone, their child may find great joy, health and success following a different course in life.

I know people whose children follow paths far different from their parents. In one case, Joe works as an information technology consultant. He works only periodically by choice, feeling that work and the money one earns should support life's more important pursuits, which in his case include organic gardening, cooking and woodworking. Dana, Joe's wife, works part-time as an interior decorator and website designer. Holding values similar to her husband's, she devotes much of her time to yoga, meditation, organic gardening, cooking and community organizing for various local ecological protection initiatives.

The couple lives simply and have faced money challenges, but they have found ways to provide for the basics and even enjoy some luxuries. They have also faced derision from Joe's father, Dominick, who worked for thirty-five years at his excavating and landscaping business before retiring last year. Dominick calls his son "lazy" and "disappointing." The disconnect between Joe and his father has long been a source of sadness for Joe and Dana.

Joe and Dana have a small home in the far northern suburbs of New York City on a lot large enough to support a summer vegetable garden, a greenhouse and a flock of six pet chickens that provide fresh organic eggs that they share with neighbors and a local food pantry.

Striving to be supportive of the varied interests of their two children, the couple marvel at the work being done by their younger child, a son who is now 25. "Paul works on Wall Street, where his first job paid $75,000 per year," boasts Joe. "Neither Paul's mom nor I have ever made that much money!" His dad goes on to describe how Paul saves and invests and seems to be all about money and the market.

"I don't know where he got that, but he's passionate about finance," says Dana.

Both parents smile broadly when they talk about how happy the world of finance and investing makes Paul, a world entirely foreign to these "live for the moment" parents. One could say that Paul has inherited his parents' zest for living, but applied this to his interest in finance, which he finds challenging and often fun.

Here's another example where the fruit in some ways falls quite a distance from the tree. While mom is a professor of social work and dad an executive in a pharmaceutical corporation, this

Ken Dolan-Del Vecchio

couple's son finds great satisfaction as a singer-songwriter and makes a subsistence-level income working at a café. He and his band have recorded two collections of songs and they are gaining a following in a cluster of towns in Northern California. He and his girlfriend, who works in a health food store, live very simply. They do not want to own a car, they have few possessions, and they seem blissfully happy. His parents look on with bemused gratitude.

His mom recently told me, "I don't know who he takes after in our family: He doesn't care about money, he never seems to worry, he's thrilled about the art he's creating, and he couldn't be happier. We're thrilled at how well he's doing."

While I started the previous paragraph with the suggestion that "the fruit in this case seems to fall far from the tree," a more accurate assessment shows that this is not the case at all. For in both of these stories the parents believe in themselves and their ways of approaching the world and they also believe in the validity of other approaches. It seems that their children, in charting independent courses for their own lives, share these beliefs. The apple doesn't fall far from the tree after all.

Key points:
1. Exceptional parents believe in themselves and others, knowing there are many paths to joy, health and success.
2. If accepting the differences between you and your child presents a great challenge, consider how you may learn to accept and embrace their different path in life. Conversations with friends, reading books and consultations with therapists can help.
3. It helps to validate the experiences, ideas, and feelings of your child even when they are very different from your own. Ask questions to learn more about what they're thinking and feeling.
4. Recognize that there is no "one size fits all" when it comes to crafting a successful life. The timing of your child's milestones,

the value he or she places on particular achievements, and his or her definition of success may vary from yours. Celebrating our child's experiences, those similar to as well as those different from our own, can be a wonderful aspect of parenting.

Think for Yourself, Decide for Yourself

"I want you to support your opinions and beliefs with facts and your own thoughts about those facts." With these words and the discussion that followed, my son Erik's eighth grade English teacher gave her students a lesson on critical thinking. She was also sharing with them one of her personal values, for not every adult believes that children, or indeed anyone, should be encouraged to think for themselves.

As a person who strives to be an exceptional parent, I agree with Erik's teacher. I see well-informed, independent thinking as a key skill for successful living and one that we should help our child develop. It's a skill that builds competence, confidence and a continuously improving ability to make good decisions. By contrast, the habit of avoiding critical thinking by unquestioningly adopting the views of others can diminish our sense of ourselves as capable and self-reliant people.

Clearly, the opinions and beliefs held by one person may differ substantially from those reached by another person. Our thinking brings us to different conclusions because personal history, family background and other experiences influence the values that shape our thinking.

As we'll discuss more later on, different perspectives are not a bad thing. Quite the opposite. They almost always occur when we risk being honest with one another, which gives us the chance to hear another viewpoint and perhaps learn something helpful from it.

When we share our values and thinking with our children, we invite them to share our critical perspectives, challenge them, and, ultimately, as they grow toward independence, create their own. Some examples:

- Disagreeing with the seemingly endless distraction presented by phones, tablets and television, a single mother, Sharon, continues her family's long tradition of 6 p.m. dinners that all household members are expected to attend with no communications technology allowed at the table. She and her two sons, Adam, 11, and Carl, 13, spend dinnertime talking over what's new in their lives and the world around them. As you may suspect, they've had some lively discussions about this "no tech" rule, but it stands to this day. Sharon has insisted that they deserve one another's full attention during this brief time together, saying how much she values being with them without any distractions. While both sons have protested in the past, more recently they've made it clear that they, too, value this family tradition. In fact, Carl recently mentioned that he keeps his phone off during lunchtime also. He said that he only puts it on when he's got a specific reason for using it, explaining "I don't want my most important relationship to be with my phone, and I like having time to pay attention to what's going on around me, think without distractions, and actually be with other people."

- Donna, a friend of mine, prizes this question: *How can we do this without buying something?* She tells me that she and her wife, Sylvia, regularly ask this question of one another and their six-year-old daughter, Emily. They started using this question several years ago after reading *Voluntary Simplicity,* a book written by Duane Elgin. It has led them to make one-of-a-kind Halloween costumes, bake exceptionally creative cookies (such as pumpkin-chocolate chip) for special events at their daughter's school, and collaborate with neighbors on home renovations, gardening projects and child care. They believe that the opportunities resulting from this simple question have enriched their family by expanding their imaginations, getting them to spend more time together in creative activities, and emphasizing the importance of working together with others, rewards that go far beyond money saved.

- Nathan, 12, giggled uncontrollably while telling his parents about a new television show his friends at school mentioned. It's called *Naked and Afraid*. He went on to describe how the show drops a man and woman, both of whom are naked, "in the middle of nowhere" and then follows them "blurring out their private parts" as they try to survive. Nathan knows how his parents feel about these kinds of shows and they all have a good laugh. This family has made a game out of bringing to one another's attention what they see as the most ridiculous features of media culture.

- Milt, a colleague of mine, and his wife, Aileen, homeschool their two young daughters, Stephanie and Valerie. They believe that traditional education moves too slowly and presumes "one size fits all" rather than providing individualized learning experiences. They also feel that too many schools emphasize memorizing over creativity and spend too little time teaching the arts, civics and the importance of spirituality. Milt and Aileen intend to let each child, when she completes eighth grade, decide whether or not to attend public high school.

- Anne recently consulted with a therapist about the interest that her son, Paul, 13, has developed in bodybuilding. "All he talks about is working out and he's always looking at himself in the mirror." She and John, Paul's father, after receiving the therapist's guidance, tell Paul that they're impressed with the way he's focused on fitness and health but also want to caution him about overvaluing external beauty. They make a point of noting the "beauty" of their neighbors who volunteer alongside them at the local food bank and others whom they consider beautiful in spirit.

- Juana and her daughter, Addy, 11, love watching *Project Runway* together, a television show that pits clothing designers against one another. They marvel at the work of the talented contestants and the knowledge of the panel of expert judges. The show also gives them the opportunity to discuss the merits of both competition and collaboration.

- While driving home after listening to a sermon in which their congregation's new leader described Hindus as "outside God's community," Bill and Lolita share their dismay. They decide to ask the leader for a meeting in order to challenge him on this statement. They tell their son, riding in the back seat, that nobody is outside God's community.

Regularly engaging our child in conversations of this sort, we can demonstrate how information from the world around us can be critically examined rather than absorbed with no questions asked. We can teach our child how to approach new information thoughtfully; consult with people whom they respect and trust, as well as other reliable sources of wisdom such as well-researched publications; and, ultimately, make their own judgments. We can equip our daughter or son to appreciate the richness of the world while also applying his or her own scrutiny. Encouraging our children to think critically about the information they receive, we prepare them to navigate the complex and confusing times that will undoubtedly continue into the foreseeable future.

Key points

1. Exceptional parents recognize the importance of independent thinking, noting the complexity of modern life and the strangeness of much of the information that we're subjected to every day.

2. Instead of taking sound-bite information at face value, we can seek to understand a topic more deeply by consulting a variety of sources, reading about it in some depth and discussing our thoughts with other informed adults, including those whose ideas differ from our own.

3. We can help our child develop independent thinking skills by inviting them into discussions about the information and values promoted by media and other sources, including school and communities of faith.

4. Helping our child think for him or herself empowers them to develop a thoughtful approach to living that can enrich their lives and protect them from adopting values and practices that may not serve them well.

Setting Goals

I will soon embark on a new life chapter, one devoted less to my current full-time work as a health and wellness executive and more to a number of projects close to my heart. These include creating a permaculture landscape (fruit trees, berry bushes and other plants that produce food, attract beneficial wildlife, and enhance soil quality) at my home in Massachusetts, writing, promoting healthy workplaces and striving to end domestic violence. My transition from the frenetic intensity of the corporate world to a more spiritually-focused life in rural New England fulfills personal goals that I have worked toward for decades. I'd like to share with you some of what I've learned along the way. The key message here: Setting priorities and goals can make your life a great adventure. Your example can also inspire your child as you teach them how to set their own goals and work toward them.

In this discussion, the question we addressed earlier —*Who owns this life?* —comes full circle, back to you. While that earlier discussion highlighted the importance of knowing that your child's life belongs to them and cannot serve as the means to fulfill your own dreams, here the message is *your life belongs to you.* And while this may

Ken Dolan-Del Vecchio

seem self-evident, I challenge you to identify five people among your family and friends whose actions consistently demonstrate a belief that their lives truly belong to them. People who own their lives radiate contentment, energy and enthusiasm. They enjoy their chosen vocation, work to make changes when this is no longer so, nurture rich and rewarding personal relationships, respond to adversity with grace and constructive action, and they inspire those around them. Almost every one of these people, should you inquire, will tell you that the keys to their success include the habits of prioritizing what matters most to them and setting personal goals accordingly.

By contrast, too many people, it seems to me, behave as though they stepped onto a conveyor belt in early adulthood and, as the years have passed, haven't allowed themselves to consider the world of possibilities beyond that conveyor. They rarely assess their job-related knowledge and skills, free-time interests and activities, and sets of friends and acquaintances. While great value may come from stability, it can also serve us well to consider new possibilities, evaluate and sometimes seize rising opportunities, expand our network of friends and contacts, and launch change when doing so will likely enrich our lives. We can learn how to take such an active approach to shaping our lives, and we can teach our child how to do the same.

For me, this knowledge grew stronger when my friend and psychotherapist colleague, Lucille Grey, attended a training that introduced behavioral health clinicians to life coaching. I was the manager of Prudential's Employee Assistance Program at the time. The life coach training program made such a positive impact on Lucille that she inspired our whole team to enroll in a certification program. The centerpiece of the program was an internship in which each of us was assigned another trainee as a coaching client. Edith, my coach, helped me clarify my vision for the future and step forward on the path that I continue today.

After our team completed the certification program, we launched life coaching as a service available to all Prudential

38

employees. Almost immediately, it became one of our most popular offerings. Almost every participant loves the coaching experience and the results they achieve. I've seen coaching clients get back on track to finish a degree in higher education, de-clutter their schedule to gain more family time, and start exercising regularly.

While it helps to work with a life coach—someone who will help you set personal goals and then lovingly nudge you to keep moving toward them—you can apply coaching's key principles on your own. They include getting to know yourself well enough to identify your top priorities, envisioning the goals you want to achieve, and taking concrete steps to get there.

You can start by asking yourself how satisfied you are, on a scale from one to five, with important aspects of your life, and recording your answers. Include your relationships with family members, spiritual well-being, overall health, educational and work achievements and financial status. Consider your results. Decide which of these aspects of life will be most important for you to pay attention to as you move forward. Envision your life as you'd like it to be at a specific time in the future *and write your vision down with as much specificity as you can muster.* (Writing our goals down increases our likelihood of fulfilling them.)

"Ten years from today, Tim and I will be living on at least ten acres, a place where I will have chickens, goats, and maybe horses and alpacas. Tim and I will enjoy an ever-deepening experience of love and mutual understanding. We will be financially secure. I will no longer be working full-time for one employer. Instead I'll be working at a variety of writing, speaking/training, and community development projects, each of which feels more like a labor of love than work. I will also have enough time to create a permaculture landscape. I will continue to nurture a close, loving relationship with Erik and will be in at least weekly contact with him no matter where each of us is in the world." This was my vision statement all those years ago. I have made some changes to it here and there, as you will likely do with yours, and it continues to describe the ideal to which I aspire.

Once you have your vision statement you can compose and then work toward the short-term goals that will move you toward it. Some examples of goals:

- I will eliminate my credit card debt by the end of next year.
- I will learn all that I can about my supervisor's role so that I'm prepared to advance to the next level at this or another workplace within the next two years.
- I will start walking for at least 20 minutes, three days per week or more, for the next three months.

The last tip before we move ahead to talk about how you can help your child with goal setting: Share what you're working toward with family members and friends who you know will help you stay at it. My friend, Rick, and I meet for breakfast monthly. When I see him two days from now he will surely ask, "Why is it taking so long for you to finish this book?"

You can help your child get started on their own path toward personal fulfillment by asking typical "coaching questions," simple inquiries that help her or him name their interests, identify what they want to achieve, and decide upon the steps that lead from here to there. You can start asking these sorts of questions when your son or daughter is very young. This can get them into the habit of asking the same questions of themselves. Some examples:

- You say you want to play baseball, soccer, and take guitar lessons this spring. That sounds like a lot to take on if you also want to have time to spend with your friends and do other fun things. Which one of those activities are you most interested in doing? Which ones would it make sense to do this coming summer or fall? Which ones could you postpone beyond then?
- You're going to be in ninth grade in September. You've talked a lot about wanting to be either an electrician or an electrical engineer when you grow up. Does one of these

still feel like a fit for you, or have you got other ideas now? Even though your goal may change, it never hurts to identify what goal draws your attention now so you can choose your classes thoughtfully. Knowing what you think you'll want for yourself in the future will become even more important as you get toward the middle of high school and start thinking about what you may want to do after you graduate.

- Since you started in college you've talked about wanting to live in Scotland. I'm excited about your passion and I'd love to help you think through how to make it happen. How are you planning to do it? What are the next steps toward getting there and what obstacles will you have to get around?

These kinds of questions can help your child develop the self-reflection and planning skills that lay the foundation for a deliberate approach to life.

When you write an email to my friend and permaculture coach, Jonathan Bates, this note will come back to you: "Please note: I've reduced my office hours for the coming year to focus on family and self-care. I look forward to responding to your email. If your question is urgent, please ALSO text me if you want to hear back within a few days."

This email comes back to all business contacts who write to him, making clear his current priorities and goals. As the parent of a three-year-old, Jonathan's declaration makes a public statement about what matters most to him.

I see great wisdom and courage here, for how many people announce to the world *on their business email* that "family and self-care" matters more than work? This may seem especially remarkable coming from a man, marking a growing trend toward more gender-equal parenting. The fact that Jonathan notes both *family* and *self-care* also shows depth of understanding, for we can only deliver our best care to others when we pay enough attention to our own.

On a practical note, his email illustrates powerful elements of the goal-setting habit we discussed earlier: writing down our objectives, sharing them with others, and recognizing that time devoted to your priority goals means time away from other activities. In this example, devoting care to self and family requires devoting less time and energy to work.

As an exceptional parent of a toddler, your priorities and goals may echo what's described above. When your child reaches his or her teens, however, their reduced need for direct care may allow you to expand your focus to include other goals. That's what happened for Erik's mom and me. When Erik was little, Lynn and I placed giving him our love and our time at the top of our priority list. As he grew more independent, progressing toward and then through his teenage years, we gradually shifted more energy toward our own long-term personal goals. For me, this meant pursuing a promotion at work, placing more emphasis on planning for semi-retirement, and spending more time on writing and speaking commitments. Similarly, Erik's mom pursued personal goals that included taking advantage of educational opportunities in line with her long-held interest in equine-assisted therapy, planning for her semi-retirement, and more frequently accepting opportunities to travel internationally for her employer. She regularly brought Erik along on travel assignments, giving him the opportunity to visit many locations across Europe.

On my 50th birthday, I brought home three 6-week-old Silver Laced Wyandotte hens, fulfilling a desire to raise chickens that started during my college years. My son, 18 at the time, enjoyed hearing about the effort I put into preparing for the birds' arrival. He asked me about my chicken books, accompanied me a couple of times when I visited people who had their own flocks, helped me set up the coop, and joined me in my excitement about the chicken's first eggs.

One day shortly after the chickens' arrival, Erik and I were standing in their enclosure watching their antics. He said, "Dad, a few of my friends have been telling me that their parents want to get chickens too. One guy said, 'yeah, my parents say they want to do lots of things like getting chickens, but your dad actually *got chickens*.'" He chuckled as he said this.

My response: "This ain't no dress rehearsal!" It's become a frequent refrain between us ever since.

When your child sees the courage and confidence you exhibit and the satisfaction you derive from working toward and achieving your goals, the example you provide can energize conversations about their own priorities and goals. As you help your child examine what they want for themselves—perhaps they want to demonstrate enough responsibility for you to feel comfortable letting them adopt a dog or cat, or excel at their favorite sport, or begin earning some money through a part-time job, or achieve the grades that will help them get into the college of their choice—you've shown by your example the importance of imagining your preferred future, setting long- and short-term goals, consistency, discipline and perseverance. This lends credence to your advice.

Whether your own goals include raising chickens, singing in Carnegie Hall (a goal recently achieved by a friend of mine who works as a human resource professional), learning a foreign language, campaigning for political office, finding time to volunteer for a cause you're passionate about, or something else entirely, you will enrich your own life and your child's life by prioritizing your goals and working toward them. Taking such a thoughtful and courageous approach to life, you offer your children the gift of knowing that they, too, can create their own blueprint for successful living. Don't be surprised when, following your example, your son or daughter dreams big and works hard to make it happen!

Key points:
1.   Setting priorities and goals can make your life a great adventure, and doing so can inspire your child to experience their own life as an adventure too.

2. You can help your child build the habits of identifying their interests, setting goals, and working toward them by asking questions that help them clarify what they want for themselves and the steps that will lead them forward.

3. While your priorities and goals will center upon your child when they are very young, as she or he gains independence during their teenage years, it makes sense to place more focus on your own personal aspirations.

4. While you may or may not work with a life coach, letting other people know your priorities and goals can help you work toward them.

5. Observing your example will reinforce for your child the importance of discovering their own personal values and priorities, and setting life goals that are in harmony with them.

6. As you move through the life cycle, your thoughtful, courageous, and energetic pursuit of personal goals will continue to inspire your child.

Chapter 2
People Habits

A person's a person, no matter how small.
—Dr. Seuss

Ken Dolan-Del Vecchio

In the 1971 classic film, *Harold and Maude,* Harold, played by Bud Cort, says to Maude, played by the late Ruth Gordon, "You sure have a way with people."

Gordon scrunches her face into her trademark crooked smile and says, "Well, they're my species."

If only it were that simple. In reality, like most everything else in life, children must *learn* people skills. This includes learning how to relate to themselves: how to make sense of their emotions and tolerate the unpleasant ones, value themselves, and balance the care they give to themselves and others. They need to learn how to manage conflict, give and receive helpful criticism, apologize when necessary, and appreciate and respect the differences among people.

As parents, it's our responsibility to help our children with it all, everything that will prepare them for a lifetime of satisfying relationships. Our own people habits, the ones that involve caring for and teaching our children, as well as those that demonstrate relationship skills through our own example, can help make this happen. This chapter explores a number of these important habits, and how we can best teach them to—and model them for—our children.

Saying No with Love and Firmness
Life inevitably includes frustration. We parents bring a degree of it into our child's life every time we say the word *no*. Exceptional parents understand that saying no can help our child stay safe, grow in judgment and maturity, honor commitments to others, grasp the difference between what they want and what they need, and learn to manage their frustration constructively. The ability to say no with love and firmness, therefore, ranks high on the list of parenting skills.

That doesn't mean that saying "no" is an easy task. Mastering the art of *no* challenges many adults, parents and non-parents alike. The key message here: Learn how to say no with love and firmness, for doing so will help your child immeasurably and also help you succeed in your own life as well.

Many years ago a family therapy mentor told me, "When you say yes or no, remember to do it like a vending machine and not a slot machine." She went on to explain, "When you ask a vending machine for something by inserting your money, the machine gives you a firm *yes* or *no*: you either get the thing you asked for or you don't (either because the machine is broken or is out of the snack you want). If you don't get the potato chips you paid for, you don't keep asking the machine over and over again by putting in more money, because you know the answer won't change."

She went on, "A slot machine, on the other hand, gives you a *yes* every now and then even though it gives you one *no* after another first. When you're playing the slot machines, *no* means *keep asking me until you get a yes*. Whether you're a parent dealing with your child or one adult talking with another, it pays to behave like a vending machine rather than a slot machine."

Exceptional parents recognize that saying no, while likely to provoke feelings of disappointment, sadness, and even anger in their child, never needs to convey hostility or lessened love. On the contrary, saying no sets a reasonable limit, something all parents must do regularly in order to help their children navigate the world. Every time we parents say no to our child, we lend them our best judgment. Therefore, we have every reason to recognize the word *no* as a gift of love.

Consider, on the other hand, the result a parent achieves when he or she behaves like a slot machine. Their child asks, "Can I (have another cookie, buy this toy, have a sleepover at Suzie's Wednesday night after school, go to the party) and Mom or Dad answers, "No," perhaps explaining their reasons briefly. The child perseveres, explaining with great feeling how badly they *need* what you have denied them. The pleas may begin rapid-fire in a retail store or while the child views the object of desire online. If their entreaties are ignored or rebutted, they progress into something like a siege, with recurring outbursts erupting whenever the parent and child find themselves together. Many parents have told me

Ken Dolan-Del Vecchio

that such barrages wear them down until they eventually give way. Against his or her better judgment, the parent's *no* morphs into a *yes* in order to gain peace and quiet.

When a parent caves in (and we've all done it), an opportunity for the child to grow in maturity has been lost. The chance for a child to learn something useful from their mom or dad—with the parent demonstrating the power of love by saying a firm no—has degraded into the experience of successfully exerting power *over* their parent, the power of domination.

Following such an inversion of authority, a number of unpleasant feelings are likely to arise. The child may feel momentarily triumphant but then confused and guilty. The parent will likely feel weakened in competence and integrity, as well as a bit resentful toward their child. Overall, the parent-child relationship has been temporarily diminished rather than enriched. It pays to do things differently.

While exceptional parents listen respectfully to their child's requests, they ultimately take responsibility for giving a decisive answer. And once that answer has been delivered, the parent does not waver or revisit their decision. If the child continues to beg and plead, the parent reminds the child of their decision and the reasons for it. The exceptional parent may then offer the child some options for positive behavior. These include thinking about why the parent said no in order to understand the reasons more fully; sitting with and perhaps sharing their feelings of sadness, disappointment, frustration, and anger (it can help to attach words to the resentment felt), and shifting their attention to something entirely different. If the pleading continues, the parent tells their child that what they're doing shows disrespect. The parent lets their child know that begging and pleading, rather than leading to a change in the parent's decision, demonstrates improper behavior.

It is important to mention that we sometimes say "no" when saying "yes" would have been a better decision. Our exaggerated worries, sometimes passed along from the families in which we grew up, often lurk behind such instances. My parents, for example, were cautious people who generally saw the potential for danger outweighing the likelihood of adventure within many of life's opportunities. For example, my brothers and I were not allowed to go to summer camp or on overnight class trips. I believe these opportunities may have helped us improve our social skills, build more and stronger friendships during our early years, and see the world as a less scary place overall.

Please keep in mind that none of us is infallible: We can allow ourselves to change our minds, including when we make decisions about setting limits with our children. It's okay to come back to your child on occasion with an "I've given this some more thought and decided that the answer is yes instead of no."

When Erik got excited about playing paintball with his friends, all I could think about was him getting his eye put out or having that happen to one of his friends. I was all about "no." Talking this through with his mom, who helped me realize that my fears were echoes from the past, I changed my mind. As it turned out, Erik loved playing paintball with his friends during their early teen years and everyone made it through unscathed.

I have seen parents say no to their child and then respond to the child's tearful appeals in a very loving fashion. I recall spending an afternoon at a carnival with a friend and her son, who was five years old at the time. The child dissolved into tears when she told him that he couldn't go on another carnival ride because we needed to leave in order to arrive on time for dinner at another friend's house. Crouching to meet him at eye level, she said to her son, "Honey, I'm sorry this makes you so sad, but we have to go now or we'll be late for dinner." As he continued to sniffle, she said, "I'm glad you had so much fun that you wanted to stay longer and I know it's frustrating to leave when you're having a great time." The little boy still looked glum, but he nodded and held his mom's hand as we walked toward their car.

My friend gave her child a reasonable limit and helped him understand the reason for doing so. She also gave him the words *sad* and *frustrating* to help him identify what he felt. Giving children words to name their feelings can help them gain self-understanding, self-control and calm.

The formula remains the same until a child grows into his or her teenage years. One caveat: as our son or daughter gains more independence, wise parents recognize that there are fewer areas of our child's life over which we hold absolute authority. We can (and should) maintain house rules that specify when our child needs to be home, when the lights get shut off, and the chores for which each family member holds responsibility. These provide a predictable structure for the household, something that benefits everyone. It makes sense to hold firm on these expectations, assigning logical consequences, such as a short period without use of the family car, when they are not met. Additionally, we owe it to our child to continue to remind them of our personal values—something we've been demonstrating and talking about already for years—when it comes to matters like dating, sex and the use of alcohol and other substances.

In most cases, however, we can no longer take full responsibility for where, with whom and how our child spends his or her time when not at home or school. It is vital to acknowledge this reality.

When it comes to the choices a teenager makes, therefore, we no longer always have the *no* option available to us. Exceptional parents recognize this and back away from trying to control that which lies beyond their control. Instead, having developed a bond with their child based on love and trust, they shift from "yes" and "no" to the fine art of *influencing*.

- 13-year-old Darren calls Joyce, his mom, from a friend's house on Saturday afternoon and says he'd like to spend a couple more hours playing paintball. Joyce, recalling that her son has a big science project due on Monday, says "That's up to you, but I'm just a bit concerned for you because you're expected to finish that project by Monday." She doesn't say, "No, you need to come home right now to do your school project." She knows this could start a power struggle that she stands to lose. Despite such a demand, her son could still saunter into the house 90 minutes later. Instead, she gives him a friendly reminder about his schoolwork. What she says may influence him to play it safe and give himself time this afternoon for his school work. He may, on the other hand, decide to spend the afternoon playing paintball. His mom leaves the decision to him. After all, the school project is his responsibility, not hers.

• 17-year-old Paula tells Sal, her father, that she and her 18-year-old boyfriend, Raj, a young man whom her parents hold in high regard, have decided to "be exclusive." Despite feeling a little faint, Sal retains enough presence of mind to say, "Wow, that sounds like a big decision. What do the two of you mean by 'being exclusive?'" Paula excitedly describes how they'll date only each other and may even get rings to celebrate their commitment to one another. Sal asks her if they're having sex.

Paula blushes. "I don't want to talk about something so private," she says.

Sal tells Paula that he's asking because he's concerned about the possibility for her to become pregnant or contract a sexually transmitted disease. He says he's sorry for making her feel uncomfortable, but at the same time he wants to make sure that she's protecting her health.

Paula says, "Dad, I know you love me and you're only trying to make sure I'm okay, but this conversation—like you said—is starting to creep me out. I'm not a little kid anymore and I know how important it is to take care of my health and safety."

Sal says, "Okay, I get it. I'm happy that you're so happy about deciding to be exclusive with Raj and I hope you continue to enjoy your relationship with him."

Ken Dolan-Del Vecchio

Later that day, Sal and Jan, Paula's mother, decide to schedule an appointment for their daughter with an ob-gyn physician so Paula can discuss reproductive health matters with an expert.

- An industrious 16-year-old has saved up $15,000 from years of baby-sitting, pet-sitting, and working summers as a server at the local ice cream parlor. While she used to talk about applying some of that money to expenses during her college years and perhaps investing some in mutual funds, this afternoon she tells her parents that she wants to spend it all on a used car. Her parents listen and acknowledge how excited she feels about the car that drew her interest. Next, they remind her of her earlier plans for the money, and also of the fact that many colleges don't allow freshmen to have cars on campus. Finally, they remind her that she's free to use either of her parent's cars when they aren't using them. They ask her to consider these points and sleep on it before making a final decision about whether or not to buy the car.

Conversations like these allow parents to respectfully point out options and lend their best judgment instead of trying to control things that, realistically, lie beyond their control. After all, saying no to a teenaged or adult child may make them feel disrespected and, as a result, even more committed to their original plan of action. Exceptional parents recognize when they encounter a parenting situation in which their child's age and developmental stage render "yes" and "no" answer less appropriate than influencing skills.

The world presents endless objects of desire and opportunities for experiences, but we cannot pursue them all. Learning to accept limits and manage the feelings that go along with them is essential. Your skill at saying no with love and firmness and, as time moves forward, your influencing skills, can equip your child for a lifetime of thoughtful responses when faced with life's inevitable frustrations and tough decisions.

Key points

1. Saying no never needs to convey hostility or lessened love. On the contrary, it is one of the most important ways to demonstrate the power of love.

2. Saying no offers your child the opportunity to learn from your judgment and grow in maturity.

3. Remember that you cannot prevent your child from facing loss and frustration, but you can help them learn how to manage their reactions.

4. Giving your child words to identify his or her feelings, such as "sad," "disappointed," frustrated," and "angry," can help them gain self-knowledge, self-control, and calm.

5. As your child grows toward adulthood, it becomes less realistic to say no and more constructive to help them identify options and develop well-informed judgments of their own. In short, exceptional parents recognize when it no longer makes sense to try to take responsibility for many of their child's decisions. They stop saying "yes" and "no" and, instead, offer positive influence.

Better Than Lecturing

Tempting as it may be to lecture your child about working hard, managing their time, paying attention, asking for help, and all the other things you want them to learn, lecturing works nowhere near as well as simply telling stories about your own life experiences—the good, the bad, and the "I can't believe I actually did that." Sharing your own missteps and what you've learned as a result makes such a strong impression because personal stories assure your child that you're with him or her in this messy, unpredictable thing called life. You're not perfect and you're not all-knowing. You have something valuable to offer, however, as a result of your lifetime of learning. The key message here: Instead of lecturing your child, share honestly about your own life.

During third grade, Erik started getting anxious about grades. He wanted to earn straight A's and became very unhappy with himself whenever he received anything less. Whenever he started talking about his worry over grades and asked for our help, we responded—*because he asked*. First, we gave him our recommendations. We reinforced the importance of scheduling an hour in the evening for homework, keeping up with his assignments, and paying close attention during class. We also reminded him that he was a great kid with strong schoolwork habits, as he was almost always already doing the things we mentioned.

What really helped him though, were the stories we told him about our own struggles with schoolwork and grades.

I have always been a bit compulsive (okay, maybe more than just a bit). Erik's mom and I both cared about grades and worked hard to do our best. Both of us, however, learned that we would not always achieve straight A's and, remarkably, the world did not crumble when the unthinkable B's, C's, and D's came to pass.

I remember telling Erik, "Grades were really important to me at first but after I got a few C's I understood that it didn't help to make myself crazy over them. I did okay, getting A's and B's most of the time, but I got a few D's and even F's on assignments throughout my school years. Some classes I did really well in and others not so much."

I told Erik about how difficult math classes were for me and how I generally fared better in science and English. Lynn joined in, telling Erik some stories from her days as a student at very strict Catholic schools in New York City. We told Erik that we both remember doing better at school when we worried less about grades and simply tried to learn about the things that interested us most, while keeping up as best we could with the rest of our subjects.

I went on to share with Erik that I ultimately did quite well in high school and graduated near the top of my class. My first semester in college, however, was another story entirely. I told Erik how thrilling it was to get to know my new friends and enjoying the freedom that came with being far away from home for the first time. I got so involved with my new social life I lost focus and nearly failed many of my courses.

Erik was surprised to learn that his parents had encountered such challenging times at school. He said, "Wow, you and mom got some pretty bad grades!" He asked questions and laughed and, as he did, we could almost see the "grades anxiety" draining out of him. After a few of these conversations, Erik's attitude toward school shifted. He became far more relaxed. He trusted that his study habits were adequate and he accepted some C's and even one or two D's without anxiety. (There were one or two occasions when his mom and I privately wondered whether he had learned this lesson *too well,* but we kept that question between us.)

While intuition, fear for their child, and family traditions cause many parents to doggedly emphasize hard work and study skills, my own experience and consultations with families that included school-aged children testifies to the importance of the approach I describe here. Incidentally, this strategy works wonders regardless of your child's age.

Through the rest of grade school, middle school and all the way to the end of his senior year in high school, Erik was able to put his grades in healthy perspective. He did well without feeling unduly stressed and received a scholarship offer from the university that he ultimately decided to attend.

When he was preparing to visit the colleges where he would apply for admission, I told him a bit more about that first semester of mine. While what I had told him years earlier about being distracted from my studies by my newfound freedom and friends were part of the story, I had left out other parts, the ones about marijuana and alcohol.

Now that he was older, I told Erik that at age 17, I had regularly smoked marijuana and drank beer, cheap wine, and brandy with my high school friends, usually on weekends. I told him that when I went away to college that habit continued. I told him, "One night toward the middle of my first semester I was 'partying' with friends in the dorm room a few doors down the hall when my stomach went haywire. Sitting on my friend Steve's bed, with his roommate Doug and our hall-mates, Julie and Frank, sitting cross-legged on the floor, I lurched forwarded and vomited. I felt sick for the rest of that night and into the next day, and, needless to say, I also felt extremely embarrassed."

"That's quite a story, Dad," Erik said, grinning.

I went on, "Indeed—that was the last time I smoked marijuana and a moment of reckoning for me regarding my drinking as well. I cut way back on my use of alcohol, and got back on track with my coursework."

Erik said, "Sounds like a turning point, Dad."

He was surprised to learn about this history because for all of his life I've rarely picked up an alcoholic drink. I told Erik that shortly after that nasty vomiting incident, I not only cut way back on my drinking, but also started working out with weights and running. Any alcohol consumption made me feel less energetic for my workouts the next day. So I stopped drinking almost entirely. To this day, I rarely drink.

In addition to telling Erik about our own adventures with substance use, Lynn and I let him know that both sides of his family include recovering and active substance abusers. We wanted him to know that addiction touches almost every family, including ours.

While most of Erik's college visits included his mom or me, he visited one without us, camping out in the dorm room of a friend who is one year older than him. Later, when I asked him what he thought of the school, Erik told me that he thought highly of the school but, "I made a mistake." He went on to describe how he went drinking with the friend with whom he stayed and his dorm buddies.

"I got so sick," he said. "I didn't puke, but I came close—I won't be drinking that much again anytime soon."

I believe that hearing his mom's and my stories over the years helped Erik feel free to share this kind of experience with me. We were able to talk his experience through without him feeling judged or embarrassed. After all, he knew I'd gotten F's, nearly failed out of college, and once became so intoxicated that I vomited in my friend's dorm room. (Of course, there is a fine line here. There are some personal stories that I will likely never share with my son. Your good judgment will help you decide where to draw that line personally.)

When speaking with your child of any age, it pays to empathize with what they're going through by letting them know that their words and the feelings attached have registered with you. When Erik shared how drunk he got while visiting his friend's college, I said, "Wow, that sounds like a nasty experience. I'm glad you stopped drinking before getting to the point of vomiting. I'm also happy that you trust me enough to tell me about it."

It can also help greatly to tell them something about your own life experience that relates to their current situation. While you don't want to imply that you understand exactly what they're going through and know how they can resolve whatever concerns they face, letting your child know that you've faced challenges similar to theirs can help them feel supported. This type of communication opens the way for further sharing, something a lecture will never accomplish.

Key points:
1. Instead of lecturing your child, share honestly about your own life.
2. Active listening and empathy, which you can demonstrate by reflecting to your child your understanding of what they've said and the feelings connected to their experience, is an essential first step for helping him or her cope with distress.
3. Lecturing attempts to assert *power over*. This implies that you see your child as less than competent and can lead to them feeling shamed rather than empowered.
4. Sharing your own stories, on the other hand, invites your child to grasp that you can relate to their situation because you've lived through similar experiences. It allows you to

offer your life lessons in a manner consistent with *power with*. As a result, your child is likely to feel empowered as well as closer to you.

The First Rule for Building Self-Esteem

"Are you stupid?" said the woman to the wide-eyed little boy, who appeared to be about 4 years old. She scoffed loudly and rolled her eyes. The boy, presumably her son, clung to the half-full shopping cart and bounced alongside as his mother pushed. He seemed to take little note of her words. I hadn't seen what happened immediately before her outburst as they had just rounded the corner into the aisle where I was searching through shelves of pasta sauce. The mom was slumped over her cart, crowding the much younger child who sat in the up-front seat, as the family moved slowly along. I couldn't help but wonder how it must feel to be so young and have "Are you stupid!" flung at you by one of the biggest, most powerful people in your world, perhaps the one person who you love more than any other.

A great deal has been written and said in recent years about the importance of self-esteem and helping our children build theirs. Exceptional parents practice a simple habit that goes a long way toward achieving this goal. Recognizing the enormous power they hold within their child's life and wanting to always assert their power as love, they take great care to avoid assaulting their child's self-esteem by making disrespectful or even derisive comments. The key message here: The best way to support your child's self-esteem is to never attack it.

Simple as this may sound, the habit of treating our child with loving respect can be challenging to practice consistently, particularly when many of us live such high pressure, time starved lives in which *behaving irritably* has for some people become the new normal. Feeling overstretched and as though we're always falling behind, and living as we do in our *power over* world, many of us sometimes dump our frustrations on those with relatively little power. Unless we take special care, our children—our least power-ful family members (unless we also have pets)—frequently become targets.

We may attack our child's self-esteem as blatantly as what I heard in the grocery store that day. Other examples of this sort include the many insults I have heard parents, mostly fathers I must admit, shout at their child while the kids *played* (supposedly for fun) one sport or another. The instances I witnessed took place mostly on the baseball and soccer fields.

I heard one father yell at his 7-year-old daughter "Look alive, Val—stop staring at your glove like an idiot!" Another father screamed across the soccer field at his 10-year-old son, "You let them get right by you! Don't be such a coward! You've gotta challenge them!"

Such name-calling pierces a child's heart. It is no exaggeration to imagine that the child will remember the names their parent called them for the rest of their lives: "stupid, idiot, coward!" In these examples, the motivation behind the attack may reflect not only the parent's overall experience of frustration and irritability, but also their misplaced desire for their child's success at sports to finally satisfy their *own* long-unfulfilled craving for glory on the playing field.

More subtle forms of attack may be no less damaging. A 25-year old man and his two young adult sisters were out to dinner with their father when the young man showed his father his new hemp wristband, which consisted of a series of complex knots and tightly woven segments. He proudly told his dad that he had taught himself how to make these and had given a couple of them to friends as well.

His dad rolled his eyes and said, "Great, my son makes bracelets." The young man said nothing in response. Later, however, after leaving the restaurant and while walking one of his sisters to her apartment, he burst into tears. He wouldn't discuss why he was upset, but she felt certain of the cause.

It's important to note that this father's comment, "Great, my son makes bracelets," emotionally assaulted his daughters as well. After all, shaming a man for making something typically associated with women lets everyone within earshot know how little the speaker thinks of women.

Parents undermine their child's self-esteem in less aggressive ways as well. One of the most common occurs when we overly manage our child's efforts. With the very best intentions, many parents hover over their child, sometimes even doing things for him or her that would have provided a valuable learning experience had the child been allowed the opportunity to complete the task independently. As we'll discuss in more depth later on, allowing your child to work hard, even when some of their struggles end in failure, can provide valuable life lessons.

Exceptional parents support their child's self-esteem by consistently showing up. Birthday celebrations, violin recitals, school plays, holiday pageants, graduations and all manner of sporting events in which a child participates means a great deal to them. Whether or not a parent attends can have a lasting impact on how they feel about themselves. Jill, a friend of mine, will always remember that her father showed up at all of her two brothers' baseball games and even coached their teams, yet never attended even one of her basketball games until she "guilted him into it." Then, when he attended her game, it made her feel queasy because "I knew he was only there because I insisted. I told him that he didn't have to come again … and he never did." She told this story looking downward and in a soft tone, one that showed her reawakened sadness. Jill said, "For the longest time, I guess I just accepted that what I did was less important than what the boys did." It would have been helpful to Jill if her father had apologized and then started attending her games as consistently as he attended his sons, regardless of her dispensation.

Exceptional parents practice another habit that benefits the self-esteem of their children and everyone else with whom they interact: They make a habit of noticing and complimenting others on their positive personality attributes, such as kindness and perseverance. They also acknowledge the efforts others make, knowing that this recognition can fuel an upward spiral in a person's self-esteem.

It works like this:

- On a trip to the grocery store toward the end of a long day when both parent and child feel tired and less than enthusiastic about shopping, the exceptional parent tells her 4-year-old son, "I like the way you keep going and keep a smile on your face even when you're kind of tired and we're doing a chore like shopping that we're not thrilled about. I like your 'can do' spirit."

- When a father watches his daughter on the baseball field, he notices the growing stretches of time during which her attention stays laser-focused on the pitcher and batter, despite being out in left field and surrounded by distractions. At the end of the game this dad says to his daughter, "Great game! It's not always easy to pay attention when you're in the outfield and I saw that you were keeping your eye on the ball most of the time!"

- A mom watches her son on the soccer field and notices that while he doesn't ferociously challenge players on the other team, when he has the ball he runs fast and passes with great accuracy to his teammates. At half-time this mom hugs her son and says, "Wow, you sprint so quickly and kick with amazing aim! That takes practice and talent. I also see you passing to your teammates. You really know what it means to be a team player!"

- After watching their 16-year-old son's performance in his high school's rendition of *Godspell,* each parent tells him what they liked best about his performance.

Verbal recognition like this means the world to children (and adults alike). The more we practice noticing the positive and bringing it to the attention of others, the more we feed their positive spiral of self-esteem. And make no mistake about it, the term *spiral* fits perfectly. Self-esteem lies at the very center of many important beliefs about ourselves, including our body image, intelligence, likeability and belief in our capacity to learn. Our belief in our ability to navigate change grows or lessens exponentially starting with the way those closest to us in childhood communicate their belief (or lack of belief) in our value and competence. The more we believe in our value as competent human beings, the more we will risk taking new challenges, see change as opportunity, and embrace our errors as learning experiences—activities that, in turn, further expand our feelings of competence. And so the positive spiral continues.

Unfortunately, the shaping influence of a parent's beliefs about a child can also move in the opposite direction. If I'm told regularly by my parents that I lack judgment, intelligence, focus, determination, and discipline, I'm less likely to seek new challenges, expect successful outcomes and welcome change.

A bit of clarification may help at this point, for some readers may wonder if I'm suggesting that exceptional parents comment only upon their children's positive qualities. Some readers may even wonder if I'm suggesting that a parent exaggerate their child's positive attributes. Not at all.

Much has been written in recent years about a recent generation of middle-class and upper-middle-class children who were raised to expect affirmation for their every move, as though simply showing up warrants a gold star and maybe even a trophy. I don't support this kind of behavior by parents, teachers, coaches, or anybody else. Unrealistically inflating a child's view of their own skills is not kind. On the contrary, distorting their view of reality in this way sets them up for problems.

Instead of showering your child with unearned, exaggerated compliments, nurture her or his developing self-esteem by rigorously avoiding personal insults and sharing reality-based compliments regarding positive aspects of their behavior. Later, we'll discuss how exceptional parents deliver constructive feedback when their child misbehaves or needs help mastering a skill.

Key points:

1. The first way to build your child's self-esteem is to never attack it.

2. Noticing your child's positive behaviors and verbally recognizing her or him on these can build a positive self-esteem spiral.

3. Do not give your child untruthful or exaggerated compliments. Doing so distorts a child's ability to accurately assess their own attributes and skills. It never helps to lessen a child's ability to grasp reality.

4. Affirming a child's self-esteem does not imply that parents should avoid providing feedback. We all benefit from constructive criticism, as long as it is offered in a manner that is encouraging rather than demeaning. More to come on this.

Truly Constructive Criticism

How many of us like to receive criticism? I can almost hear your response! I don't know of anyone who enjoys being corrected. Children feel no different from adults in this regard, and exceptional parents keep that in mind. They approach the delivery of criticism with care and sensitivity. Because the things that others do and say can evoke strong negative reactions, exceptional parents develop skill at putting a bit of distance between the words that pop into their heads and the words that come out of their mouths. They craft what they have to say in accordance with their goal of helping their child learn, achieve greater success and feel even more competent. The key message here: Exceptional parents make a habit of delivering constructive rather than destructive criticism.

What's the difference? Essentially, constructive criticism identifies specific behavior that works against the child's success, lets the child know why that behavior has to go, describes what more effective behavior looks like, and conveys a belief in the child's ability to make the change.

Here's a simple formula for delivering constructive criticism: "When you did A (a specific behavior), that wasn't the best choice because B (the negative impact of the behavior). In the future, I'll expect you to demonstrate C (the preferable specific behavior)." Some examples:

- When you reached across Grandma's plate to grab the ketchup, that was not okay because your sleeve almost fell in Grandma's mashed potatoes and it's also not good table manners. Next time you need something that you can't reach, I'll expect you to politely ask a person who can reach it to pass it to you.
- When you interrupted your sister while she was telling her story that was rude because everyone should be allowed to finish what have to say. It's important to respect other people by listening to them and letting them finish before responding. I'll expect you to do that next time.
- When you pushed your little brother that was not okay. You could have hurt him and, in this family, we only touch each other in ways that show love. From now on, I'll expect you to touch your little brother by giving him a hug or a pat on the head or in some other way that shows kindness.

Destructive criticism, on the other hand, is received as an indictment of the recipient's character or a broadly stated complaint without any clear suggestion for improvement. This kind of criticism doesn't get specific about the behavior that should change, doesn't provide a reason why the current behavior doesn't work, and gives no clear prescription for new behavior. Instead, it comes across as a personal attack.

Destructive criticism often includes the words *always* and *never*, along with descriptions that deliver opinion rather than observable fact. Rather than point toward a solution, what was intended as a correction strikes the recipient as character assassination. Destructive criticism hurls labels like *rude, nasty, childish, uncaring, ignorant*, words just one step away from name-calling, and they usually have a similar impact.

Some examples of destructive criticism:

- You're always so rude at the dinner table. You have no manners at all.
- You never let people finish what they are saying. It's all about you!
- You act like a monster toward your little brother. One day soon he'll be strong enough to fight back and you'll end up with a broken nose.
- You have no common sense!
- You're always running away from reality!

If you keep a level head, avoid lashing out in anger, and speak with your goal in mind—the goal of helping your child learn how to behave in a more positive fashion—you will deliver truly helpful criticism.

Key points:
1. Nobody likes to give or receive criticism, so don't be too hard on yourself if you find this topic a particularly difficult one to approach.
2. Truly constructive criticism does not insult or demean the recipient. Instead, it offers them an opportunity to learn something valuable.
3. A simple and effective formula:
   - Describe the behavior you witnessed that you'd like to see change.
   - Identify the negative impact of the behavior (the reason a change makes sense).
   - Describe the positive behavior that you'd like to see.

Ken Dolan-Del Vecchio

Welcoming Conflict

What if we expected people to have different perspectives on the same situation, different answers to the same questions, and different understandings of the same words? In short, what if we expected conflict and embraced it as a learning opportunity instead of a source of pain? I believe we'd save ourselves a great deal of grief. Hence, this discussion's key message: Exceptional parents expect conflict whenever people share honestly, and they welcome it as an opportunity for learning and building closeness.

I recall two experiences that taught me how simple it *can* be to face conflict, as well as the potential costs of avoiding it. The first took place in a small consultation room at Regent Hospital, the psychiatric inpatient hospital in Manhattan where I'd landed my first real job in the behavioral health field. I worked as a mental health counselor. That meant I met with my assigned patients once a day to learn how they were doing and provide them with support, encouragement and as much guidance as I could muster at age 22 armed with a bachelor's degree is biopsychology. Because of our newness to this kind of work, each of us who worked as a mental health counselor was closely supervised by the psychiatric social workers and psychiatrists who led the treatment team.

Three weeks into my new job, two of the other counselors and I met with a senior social work clinician and the chief psychiatrist to share updates on our assigned patients. While I don't recall the specific content of the conversation between one of the counselors and the chief psychiatrist, I'll always remember the conversation's tone. The counselor, a twenty-something like me, after hearing what the psychiatrist proposed as the next step in a patient's treatment plan, looked the good doctor in the eye and said, "I disagree with what you're suggesting and here's why." He then elaborated upon his own ideas about the patient's current condition and needs, assertively describing his recommendations for treatment, which differed substantially from the psychiatrist's. The psychiatrist leaned forward and listened carefully.

After a brief pause, he said, "You're making some good points and helping me look at this differently. I really appreciate your insights." The two went back and forth, sharing their ideas—a memorable demonstration of *power with*.

I watched, transfixed, as these two people who completely disagreed traded opposing ideas in the friendliest fashion imaginable. Each remained positive, calm, and respectful. Their disagreement didn't drive them apart. Instead, talking through their differing viewpoints with one another seemed to increase their mutual respect and trust. I had never seen anything like it before.

In the family in which I grew up, differing opinions meant that one of two things would likely happen next: tense silence or all-out war. Caught up in the *power over* mindset that still governs most human relationships—particularly when we aren't consciously trying to challenge it—my parents, like many other people, generally greeted open disagreement as though it meant rebellion: a personal insult to their judgment and intellect. Between the two of them, this typically led to periods of cold silence, sometimes long ones, as my mother told me with much sadness one day shortly after my father had died.

When one of my parents disagreed with one of their children and we didn't back down promptly, Mom or Dad would angrily impose their point of view. They would say "You don't know what you're talking about!" or "You're just showing your ignorance!" These experiences gave me my first formula for dealing with conflict: avoid it if you can because facing it will probably get ugly. The problem with avoidance, of course, is that it creates distance and makes it impossible to come to a shared understanding.

This brings us to my second story, one told many years ago by Monica McGoldrick, my family therapy mentor. A young couple consulted with Monica because they found themselves encountering one difference of opinion after another. They had different ideas about where they should buy their first home, how much money they ought to save from their paychecks, and whether they would adopt a dog or cat. While they navigated each difference of opinion respectfully, arriving at reasonable compromises, the young woman felt increasingly distressed. She told Monica that she wondered if she and her husband had made a mistake in marrying. She took their different ideas as mounting evidence of incompatibility, noting that "my parents lived in absolute harmony—as far as I could tell, they never once disagreed during more than 35 years of marriage."

Monica paused after sharing the young woman's comment. Then she continued, "I remember feeling so very sad for this young woman's parents because if what she said was true, they lived all that time together and never really even got to know one another."

While it felt unfamiliar and, therefore, particularly uncomfortable, the young couple who sought Monica's assistance was doing all the right things. They were baring their differences, walking together through the uncomfortable terrain of negotiation, and crafting solutions acceptable to both. This forthright approach to conflict resolution, by the way, makes a key contribution to any couple's experience of intimacy, which is the willingness to risk being vulnerable, honest and trusting with one another.

Human beings will never have identical thoughts, feelings, and perspectives regarding much of anything. Our honestly stated differences don't need to trouble us, however. As my former colleagues at Regent Hospital taught me, our differences can instead become auspicious meeting places. They can become our points of connection. In the light of our differences, we learn more about how we view the world, what we believe, even who we truly are. We learn similar things about those with whom we share differing points of view. Ultimately, the bridges we build across our differences with others help us grow into our wiser, more mature selves.

We may, of course, face times when saying what we think or feel provokes anger in another person. Anger is not a bad thing when it's expressed without hostility or threat. Like other emotions, when we talk our anger through with civility and mutual respect we stand to can gain shared understanding—even when that understanding brings us to a resolution where we'll agree to disagree. We won't get anywhere, however, when one person's anger escalates into shouting, personal insults, or threats. When that happens, the following steps can help:

- In a calm voice, identify what's going on: "I can see that you're angry, and I'm going to ask you to talk with me with a normal decibel, polite tone so we can figure this out together." Doing this alerts the other person, who, for the sake of this example we'll say is your 13-year-old son, that he is indeed escalating, something he may not be fully aware of. Pointing this out and asking him to calm down often does the trick.

- If he complies, then you can talk about what's going on that makes one or both of you angry: "I know that you want a ride to Mark's house but I'm in the middle of something right now and can't do it. Let's talk about when I may be able to take you."

- If your son or daughter doesn't calm down, plan B breaks the action: "You can either take a few deep breaths and settle down or take a walk or do something else that will help you get yourself calm and then we can talk this through." It's important to say this in a calm, firm voice, the voice of *power with*. If you try to outshout your child, you will join them in a *power over* struggle that may escalate further.

- If your child is a teenager or older, after giving them options it makes sense to back away from them for a bit of time: "I'm taking a break from this conversation, let's get back together in 10 minutes (or another time that works for both of you)."

- If this angry conflict involves a very young child and he or she escalates into a full-throttle tantrum you may need to physically calm them, as I'll describe in a later section.

- After resolving the conflict at hand, it makes sense to talk with your child about how to better manage their anger: "One of the things I've learned is that anger usually has a whole bunch of other feelings seething underneath it, like disappointment, frustration, embarrassment, helplessness, humiliation and fear. It can help to think about that when you start getting irritated. Those underlying feelings are more specific that anger, so once you've got an idea of what they are it gets easier to figure out what to do next. You almost always end up feeling better than if you just let your anger grow."

All that good stuff said, who among us hasn't shouted "shut up!" or "watch your damn tone!" at our child? I know I have. It sometimes works in the short term, too: We stun them into silence. When we do that, however, we lose a teaching opportunity. It never hurts, therefore, to pull ourselves together, resume being the adult, and re-engage. We can apologize for our outburst and, a bit later, after things have calmed down entirely, invite our son or daughter into a conversation like the one described above that will help them make better sense of their anger and manage their feelings more constructively.

Exceptional parents accept the inevitable conflicts that arise within their relationships with their children, recognizing these as the positive consequence of honest communication. I recently got together with, Celine, a friend from college who I'd not seen in years. She shared with me a recent conversation with her 15-year-old daughter, Roslyn. Roslyn now has a steady boyfriend, a development that has raised a fair amount of concern for both of her parents. Celine reported how she told her daughter her fears.

"I told her that sex is such a powerful force. It's hard to resist at any age, and the consequences are big!"

Roslyn said, "Mom, why are you so worried about me having sex? I'm not ready to have sex and I'm not going to do it until I feel ready and I don't see that happening anytime soon! What was it like when you lost your virginity, anyway? Did you have a trauma or something?"

Celine recalled, "Her question really made me think. I told her the truth, which is that losing my virginity was a great experience. I was in my first year of college and dating a guy who was so much fun. He really respected me, too. We had some trouble figuring out how to make everything work together down there. I remember the tenderness we both felt toward one another and the laughter—we laughed and laughed." She smiled at the memory.

"I told my daughter all about that experience, letting her know that I'd love to imagine that her first time will be as loving and fun and safe as mine."

My friend went on to tell me that she and her daughter laughed and hugged. She feels the conversation brought them closer to one another, and she felt calmed and reassured by what her daughter had to say.

As I listened, I couldn't help but wonder where this point of conflict with her daughter may have gone if the two of them had backed off in silence, or if my friend had started lecturing instead of moving into the frank conversation she shared with me.

Differences in thinking, perception, and belief happen all the time, making conflict a predictable feature of everyday life. Exceptional parents know that addressing conflict with an open mind and heart will bring the best results. As we'll explore later on, embracing differences of all kinds will yield similar positive outcomes.

Key points:

1. Exceptional parents expect conflict whenever people share honestly, and they embrace it as a learning opportunity.
2. Addressing conflict in this way has the potential to enrich the relationship between you and your child, while avoiding conflict creates distance and makes resolution, and true intimacy, impossible.
3. It is important to enter discussions of differences with a positive, calm, respectful tone. If you approach conflict with a

great display of urgency and emotion those feelings steal the focus and make it more difficult to understand and resolve the conflict.

Finding the Strength to Apologize

When we apologize after making an error, we demonstrate strength rather than weakness. Many people seem confused about this, perhaps because we so rarely see public figures apologize. In the wake of bad behavior, those in the public eye more typically issue a torrent of denials, justifications, and attempts to change the subject. Most of us probably agree that attempts to justify an obvious mistake only damages credibility. I find myself imagining how differently certain politicians and others who have gained notoriety would be remembered had they found the strength to claim responsibility for their mistakes and then honestly work toward making things right.

Exceptional parents know the way this works. They know that maintaining personal integrity means taking responsibility for their errors. The key message of this discussion: Find the strength to sincerely apologize after you have made an error. Doing so clears the path toward restoring your credibility, along with any relationships wounded by your mistake.

Although I try to be an exceptional parent, I also regularly make mistakes. I have apologized to my son on several occasions and never once regretted doing so. I do not believe in spanking but, when he was a toddler, I once swatted Erik on his behind because he wouldn't stop doing something that I found aggravating. That "something" is lost to my memory but the swat I gave him stays with me. It was the first and only time I struck him and I apologized immediately. (Erik now refers to this moment by saying "Remember when you used to beat me?")

My apologies have served us both well, as I'll elaborate on more later, and they have also allowed Erik to learn the benefits of apologizing when applicable within his own relationships.

Somewhat regularly, I find myself advising business leaders on the benefits of apologizing, and, because there are important similarities between leading a work team and leading a family, I'll share one such story. Roberta, a hard-driving executive, had held her current post for a little more than a year. I was introduced to her by Dan, the human resources professional who supported her business group. Dan informed me that he and Pat, Roberta's supervisor, were planning to meet with Roberta because six of her 10 team members had complained that they feel unappreciated, disrespected, and largely dismissed by their boss. These employees described Roberta cutting them off before they were done speaking, pressuring them to turn assigned work in earlier than the previously agreed-upon deadlines, and walking by them in the morning without a word of acknowledgment while showering "Hello" and "How'd it go yesterday?" upon other members of the team who seemed to be her favorites.

These ignored team members said Roberta's behavior made them feel that she didn't believe they were capable of succeeding. Dan went on to tell me that Roberta actually acknowledged this sentiment. She said that those who complained were "plodding and complacent."

"Our client," Dan said, "is a give-work-your-every-waking-moment kind of employee, and she had been expecting the same from her team members. She hasn't got much people management experience and that's showing." Dan went on to say, "Roberta's own boss, Pat, by the way, told her in no uncertain terms that her standards are unreasonable within a workplace committed to encouraging employees to pursue a healthy, balanced life. Pat told her that she—Roberta—is the source of this problem, not these six team members."

Pat and Dan had scheduled a meeting for the following week that would include the two of them, Roberta, and Roberta's team. They wanted my guidance on how that meeting should play out for maximum benefit.

I gave the following recommendations:

- Use this meeting as an opportunity for Roberta to apologize to her group and commit to behaving differently from now on.
- Prepare Roberta by helping her empathize with the team members who have complaints. (In order for an apology to be effective it has to come from a sincere understanding of how our behavior has negatively affected others, and we need to regret having made this kind of impact. I advised Pat and Dan that I would help Roberta if this proved difficult for them to accomplish.)
- Help Roberta understand that the way forward begins with an apology for her unpleasant, disrespectful and demoralizing behavior.
- Send Roberta to me directly so I can coach her on the details.

As I spoke with Roberta a few days later, it became clear to me that Dan and Pat had done their job well. Roberta told me that she was gathering her thoughts for what exactly she would say during the meeting and welcomed my input. She had a couple of pressing questions, however—the same ones I've heard many times from people in her situation: Would apologizing make her appear weak? Would it diminish her power as a leader?

I assured Roberta that the result of her apology would be exactly the opposite of what she feared. Apologizing would signal to her team that she has the strength to acknowledge something true of all human beings: we make errors. Apologizing in a way where she laid out the details of her troubling behavior, along with what she has learned about its effect upon others, would open the way for the team to experience with her a new beginning. Laying out her understanding of the impact of her behavior upon others would also allow Roberta to ask her team members for clarification: Does it sound like I really understand how my interruptions and the way I added pressure to deadlines made you feel and got in the way of you doing your best work? If not, can you please tell me more about that?

The meeting took place a few days after our coaching session. By all accounts, it went very well. Roberta did an admirable job apologizing, taking full responsibility, and detailing the way her behavior affected those on the receiving end. She was surprised by what greeted her on the other side of her apology: acceptance, forgiveness, and even a hint of increased respect. One member of her team said, "It takes a big person to say what you've said, and if you follow through with what you tell us you'll do differently it'll be a great thing for us all."

Follow through, of course, makes all the difference. Apology lays the cornerstone for the building of a new history, but that's all. The person who apologizes must make that new history come alive during the days and months that follow. Anything less and their gracious words lose their value. Worse yet, their words become a reference point for hypocrisy.

How does this story apply to parenting? The skills of exceptional organizational leadership overlap considerably with those of exceptional parenting, and the willingness to apologize when we've made a mistake stands as a case in point.

It pays for parents to apologize for their small, everyday mistakes as much as for the really big ones. Let me give you some examples of each.

It's something how particular moments stick in our memories. I remember one in which Erik was probably 8 years old. He was strapped in the back seat as I drove along to complete one errand or another. Erik had a habit of telling his mom and me the plots, in great detail, of books that he read and movies he watched. At this moment, he was enthusiastically recounting such a story and had been chugging along at it without pause for probably ten minutes.

Without warning, I found myself barking, "Erik, can you be quiet for a minute? You've been going on and on and I need some peace and quiet!"

Immediately, I felt terrible. After glancing into the rearview mirror and seeing my little boy's forlorn and confused expression, I felt even worse.

"Erik," I said, "I'm sorry. That was not a nice thing to say and I apologize for it. I got sidetracked with a thought about something and I'm going to put that aside so you can finish telling me your story. Now, where did you leave off before I so *rudely* interrupted?" I said "rudely" in an exaggerated, comic tone.

His pouty expression brightened, and he giggled. Momentarily, he was off and running again, continuing his story with all his usual enthusiasm.

While this conversation is seared into my memory, Erik has no recollection of it. I'm grateful for that. I believe that my apology saved him from a moment that, if it had become a pattern, could have eroded his self-esteem. Such is the power of apology when it comes to the everyday, small aggressions that each of us commits now and then—things that could wound our child if we don't apologize for our misstep and put things back on a positive track. Here's a simple formula for making an apology:

1. Recognize when you've done something hurtful and stop doing it.
2. Gather a sense of what it must have been like to be on the receiving end of your unpleasant behavior.
3. Say "I'm sorry for (name whatever it was you did). I imagine it made you feel (sad, humiliated, dismissed, angry) and I regret having done that to you." You may also ask for a bit of clarification: "Am I right about having made that sort of impact? Are there other reactions you can share that will help me better understand how what I did affected you?" Pay close attention to the other person's response.
4. Say "I'm not going to do this again."
5. Honor the commitment you've made and follow through.

Growing up, my two older brothers and I would regularly punch, pinch, and shove each other as we rode in the back seat of our parents' car. (At the time, I thought this was normal behavior— I've since come to wonder about that assessment.) Many times, my father would react to this commotion by shouting at us to "Stop it!" and "Shut up and keep your damn hands to yourself!" At times, he would ramp up his response to "You kids spoil everything!" This became something my father said to us regularly, so much so that one of my brothers has since told me that Dad's refrain had a lasting impact on him. Taking my father's "You kids spoil everything!" accusation to heart, my brother confessed that it made him feel as though we were an unwanted burden.

Thinking about this today, I wonder how these words may have registered differently if Dad had simply apologized for them after he calmed down. I also wonder if he would have said them so frequently had he taken stock of their possible impact the first time, and then apologized.

Apology, you see, doesn't just make an impact upon the recipient; it also serves as a powerful lesson for the one who apologizes. For most of us, apologizing makes an emotion-laden impression. Few people find it easy to say, "I'm sorry." And having to say it leaves an impression on the one who does so—a deep and lifelong one for me, at least, when it comes to a situation such as the one I described, in which I needed to apologize to my son. Even today, I feel a little sad and regretful when I think of it. On the bright side, it put me on the lookout for my impatience and frustration, reinforcing my commitment to not dump my upset feelings on my son or anybody else. The merit to be gained here: if apology hurts, the pain can motivate us to learn how to avoid saying and doing things that will require more apologies. This has proven true for me, and I hope it does for you as well.

Sometimes, parents, being human, do things that hurt in a very big way, things far more potentially damaging than a few thoughtless words spoken in momentary lapses of judgment. Addiction, parental abandonment, domestic violence and other criminal behavior fall into this category. All of these break relationships and traumatize children in ways that can only be healed by transformative behavior on the part of the parent.

Apology can serve as the beginning of such transformation. As we've discussed, sincere words of apology can mark the turning point between pain-inflicting past behavior and relationship-healing future behavior. If delivered with sincerity, a full claim of responsibility and a willingness to hear the details of how our behavior has affected our loved ones, the possibility of forgiveness (or at least acceptance) grows. When a great deal of pain has been inflicted by our wrong, it may help to craft and deliver the apology with the support of professional helpers as well as loving friends and family.

Each of us makes mistakes, sometimes small and sometimes large. That's part of being human. Exceptional parents know that what we do in the aftermath of our mistakes makes a big difference. Acknowledging an error with words of apology, taking responsibility for the impact we've made upon others, and doing our best not to repeat our wrongs—these actions mark the path of strength, redemption, and healing.

Key points:
1. Find the strength to honestly apologize after you have made an error. Doing so begins the work of restoring your credibility and healing the relationships wounded by your error.
2. This applies to small mistakes as well as more significant ones.
3. The goodwill often gained through apologizing must be followed by a change in your behavior in order to prove meaningful. Apology without follow-through equals hypocrisy.
4. When planning to apologize for a substantial mistake—on the scale of abuse or criminal behavior—professional guidance and the support of loving friends and family members can prove valuable to everyone involved.

Respecting Your Child's Other Parent
As you're well aware, many marriages and other intimate relationships into which children are born or adopted do not weather

the tests of time. Parents part ways for many reasons and their parting can launch extraordinary grief, consume a great deal of money and energy, and extend across a period of time that feels—to both parents and children—like eternity.

Some parents do not legally separate, but nonetheless leave their intimate partnership behind. Their marriage persists in name only and the cohabitation that lingers may resemble anything from friendly roommates sharing a home to hostile combatants in a cold war-style standoff. Whatever the family situation, of course, children deserve protection from the stress of the disagreements parents have with one another. Beyond that, children deserve assurances that both of their parents have their best interests at heart, provided, of course, that this is true. (Unfortunately, some parents abuse or neglect their children and these circumstances must be addressed realistically by the other parent. I'll say more about this later on.)

Let me start by sharing some ideas for helping children feel supported through the challenges they face when their parents separate and divorce. Throughout this ordeal, exceptional parents never lose sight of their child's needs. They recognize that, unless their co-parent has been abusive, neglectful, or entirely absent, their child needs the love and support of *both* parents as well as any other adults who have played a parent-like role in their child's life. This may include grandparents, godparents, aunts, uncles, cousins, and neighbors who have become "like family." The exceptional parent regularly voices their respect and admiration for the role such people play in their child's life and the value their child places upon them. This starts at the moment parents announce to their child their forthcoming separation:

- "While the two of us will no longer be living together, we both love you with all our hearts and will take care of you as we always have."
- "Sometimes, parents decide they can't continue to live together and stay married but that doesn't change how much

Ken Dolan-Del Vecchio

they love their child. It doesn't change the way we'll work together to be the best parents you could possibly have."

- "We will always respect one another and stay partners when it comes to taking care of you. That will never change."

Messages like these give short-term reassurance, but it takes follow-through to make it real. Below are some examples of what that looks like:

- Absolute consistency with child support and alimony payments. In situations where alimony applies, the payer must keep in mind the benefits for their child. Specifically, a co-parent who receives enough income to support themselves feels less stress and can therefore devote more energy to caring for their child.

- Kindness and respect voiced to, and about, your ex. This conveys to your child that you have faith in their other parent's competence and parenting skills, which helps your child to feel more secure.

- Never asking your child to report on their other parent's behavior. This offers your child many benefits. As we discussed above, it conveys respect for the other parent's competence and is therefore reassuring to your child. It also conveys respect for your co-parent's privacy, which at the same time teaches your child about the importance of your privacy, and their own as well. Finally, imagine for a moment what it would be like to be in your child's position. How would it feel to be expected to spy on one parent for the other? How would this make you feel about both parents? How would it affect your overall level of stress? As you grew toward adulthood, what would this experience have taught you about the use of surveillance as a way to control your intimate partner?

- Communicating directly with your child's other parent about matters involving your child, rather than asking the child to carry messages on your behalf. A child who knows that his

80

or her parents maintain direct contact, reach consensus, and provide consistent parenting, knows a kind of security that all children deserve.

- Staying enthusiastically involved with your child's life. This means being aware of their changing likes, dislikes, hopes, and dreams; regularly spending time with them; giving lots of undivided attention, and listening carefully to what they have to say. Your sincere engagement and emotional support will strengthen your child and be remembered always.

The examples above hold importance also for parents who live under the same roof, whether or not they enjoy an intimate relationship. Exceptional parents respect the boundary that surrounds their relationship as a couple and as collaborative adults. They talk directly with one another rather than through third parties (including their child), work their conflicts out with civility, make joint decisions about parenting and communicate those decisions with consistency.

Exceptional parents also nurture a person-to-person relationship with their child. They know their child directly through a deep personal connection built upon years of caregiving, conversation and shared experiences. They share reports with their partner about their child. But they don't rely upon their partner to communicate for them or otherwise try to create their relationship (or, more accurately, the illusion of a relationship) with their child.

At the start of this discussion I mentioned something that occurs with uncomfortable frequency: parental neglect and abuse. Examples include:

- Leaving a young child alone without adult supervision.
- Taking a child to inappropriate places such as bars and settings where illegal substances are being used.
- Verbal, emotional, sexual or physical abuse.

I don't want to cause alarm, but I'd be remiss without elaborating a bit more on this topic. When a child tells stories that suggest neglect or abuse by the other parent (or any other person, for that matter), first of all, *believe them*. As casually as possible, ask for more details. Depending upon the severity of what your son or daughter describes, you may decide to bring the matter directly to their other parent or first consult with one of your trusted confidants or a helping professional. At the very least, talk over what you've heard from your child with a confidant who can help you decide what to do next.

Remember also that clear accounts of abuse or neglect require reporting to the official local agency responsible for child protection. If the situation warrants such reporting, I strongly recommend a prompt meeting with a therapist for assistance in bringing the matter to these authorities.

The most important element in these situations is the first one I mentioned: listening carefully to your child and taking what they have to say seriously, despite what may be a strong impulse to minimize or deny what you're hearing. Your child's safety may hinge upon your prompt attention to what they have shared with you. Enough said on this topic.

Exceptional parents who are divorced and living apart continue to raise their child with love and devotion equal to that of couples who are intimate partners and share a home. In many cases, their child fares as well or better than many children whose parents live together.

Sandra and Charles, a couple I know well, have been divorced since their son, Josh, now a thriving young adult, was 4 years old. Sandra and Charles have stayed in tight communication as co-parents. They tell the story that follows about visiting their son's fifth-grade teacher on "Back to School Night."

After the parents introduced themselves and sat down across from her, Josh's teacher said, "Before we start talking about his schoolwork, which, by the way, is excellent, I have to tell you something. Josh apologized to me a couple of days ago because he forgot his homework at Dad's house. I was confused for a minute because

I had no idea that the two of you are divorced. I usually know, because there's a certain kind of attitude—an uncertainty, a bit of insecurity—that kids who have divorced parents often seem to have. Josh has none of that. He's a secure and happy kid. Whatever you're doing, I applaud you."

Sandra and Charles agree that this teacher's kind words were among the best gifts they've ever received.

Key points:

1. When ending their couple relationship, exceptional parents continue to place their child's needs for security, consistency, and the love of both parents as their top priority. Your support and affirmation of your co-parent helps them to care even more effectively for your child.

2. When a child describes abuse or neglect, take their report seriously and gather more information. If you have concerns for the child's safety, promptly consult with a therapist or counselor.

3. Many exceptional parents are not married to one another. They consistently communicate with one another about their child's care, always interact respectfully, keep to their agreements regarding visitation and child support, and give their daughter or son all the love and care that every child deserves.

Every Touch a Loving Touch

What if violence truly became every society's and every individual's last resort for dealing with conflict? Almost everyone, from leaders at the highest levels to ordinary citizens, claims nonviolence as their guiding philosophy. But even the most casual observation unmasks a different truth. In the real world, whether a conflict involves "friends," neighbors, intimate partners, police officers and the citizens they've sworn to serve and protect, nations, people of different faiths, skin colors, or some other distinction—indeed, even when the conflict lies entirely within the soul of one person—how likely will the story end in battering, gunfire, murder, suicide, war, or some combination of these?

We raise our children with violence going on all around us and, all the while, we hear messages that justify or minimize:

- He shouldn't have dressed like a hoodlum.
- She should have obeyed the police officer.
- We only target enemy combatants.
- She was hit by friendly fire.
- You should have known what to expect if you got me angry!
- They offended God.

Unfortunately, we have created a cruel world in which violence has become too normal. Exceptional parents harbor no illusions here. They see through the lies and justifications and stand against this madness. They recognize that violence, as Martin Luther King Jr. and others have said, only begets more violence, and do all they can to bring about a new world that promises all of our children a safer future. Their commitment often begins with a vow to make every touch to another human being a loving touch, and this shows in the ways they touch their child with their hands and words.

As with other matters we've discussed, the *how to* here may seem simple at first, but then challenging to make real in our lives. When we see violent responses to conflict at every turn, it becomes easy to deem violence the ready solution. Nonviolent options, on the other hand, require more thought and creativity.

An honest look at how we, and those closest to us, have taken the violence of the world into our own moral code may bring this point home with uncomfortable clarity. We may discover that our readiness to strike our child finds its roots in personal history that includes our own parent's use of physical punishment against us. Spanking, therefore, seems the way to teach a lesson because it has long been the most familiar option. Similarly, some of us may find it hard to remain civil toward our intimate partner when we face conflict because we long ago swallowed the belief that people of our gender deserve "head of household" status. We may not question our deeply ingrained sense of entitlement because we have for so long taken it for granted.

If any of the above rings true for you, know that you do not have to carry these legacies forward. You can change. Much has been written to help adults transform such thinking and behavior, including my previous book, *Making Love, Playing Power: Men, Women, and the Rewards of Intimate Justice*. You, your child and, indeed, all of your loved ones will benefit if you read, consult with a coach or therapist, and do whatever else it takes to challenge such beliefs and start consistently treating others with civility and respect.

Some readers may find themselves wondering how they would ever manage to instill discipline, respect, and positive values without slapping, spanking, shouting at or threatening their child. Please know that verbal and emotional abuse rank high on the scale of violence. Many survivors of child abuse and intimate partner abuse, in fact, remember cruelty inflicted with words as hurting more than the physical assaults they endured.

An important fact to grasp here: violence does *not* help human beings learn discipline, mutual respect, and other values that most of us would consider positive. Violence may bring short-term compliance—rather than suffer a beating, most people will do as they're told in the moment. In the long run, however, violence teaches children fear, distrust, resentment, self-loathing and the perpetuation of violence in order to gain power for oneself later on.

Parents and other role models can instill self-discipline, love and respect for self and others, safe handling of delicate property, and other constructive behaviors in children far more effectively through nonviolent means, and with none of the aforementioned negative lessons coming along for the ride.

I've discussed in other places in this book the importance of adults expecting conflict and responding to it with civility. Doing so in the presence of your child provides invaluable role modeling. It's important to keep in mind that *all* children —because of their early stage of development—demonstrate unfortunate behavior sometimes. When it comes to directly managing our child's undesirable behaviors, many nonviolent strategies apply:

- Holding instead of hitting: Very young children sometimes push, shove, and punch with their hands, elbows and feet when tired, frustrated, angry, embarrassed or disappointed. They are not *misbehaving*. They simply don't know any better and are demonstrating normal infantile behavior. You can help them learn self-control by holding them in such a way that stops the lashing out and restores calm. You may have to hold tight for several minutes while they quiet. Don't say much while holding them until they calm down, as you do not want to reward their use of violence. Once the child has remained quiet and calm for a few moments and you have felt their body relax, then you can release your grasp. Now, as they remain calm, you may soothe with words that reward them for regaining self-control.

- Using words instead of whacks, echoing and reinforcing our previous discussion on constructive criticism. Whatever you may feel inclined to communicate by striking a child can more productively and precisely be communicated using words:
  — "I've already told you *no* and if you ask me one more time you will need to take some time out."
  — "Please stop picking your nose. Let me show you how to blow your nose into a tissue."
  — "Don't pat your baby sister so hard. How do you think that feels to her? (Then you demonstrate how to handle the baby very gently.)

- Giving constructive instead of punitive consequences, thereby redirecting young minds away from negative choices and toward positive ones. For example:
  — A child draws with her crayon on the hallway wall. Her mother shows her how to clean the surface and gives her

the task of finishing the cleanup job while mom supervises. When she finishes the job, mom and daughter spend time coloring together in one of the child's coloring books.

— A little boy starts crying loudly as the family dines out. His father tells him that he can either quiet down so that other people can enjoy their dinner or he'll have to leave the restaurant and the two of them will wait outside while the rest of the family finishes eating. If the boy doesn't quiet down immediately, the father follows through exactly as promised. Before their next planned dinner out, these parents let their son know that if he doesn't think he will be able to remain quiet at the restaurant, he will eat at home with a child-sitter. They make arrangements accordingly.

• Approaching mistakes as learning opportunities:
  — People of all ages can become open to new learning upon recognizing they've done something incorrectly.
  — Our openness to new learning depends greatly upon the attitude of the authority figure who corrects us.
  — When we, the authority in our child's life, see our child's mistake as a learning opportunity rather than a shaming opportunity, their willingness to learn will likely soar.

• Praising positive behavior: "Catch" your child doing good things. Praise reinforces positive behavior, self-esteem, and the loving bond between you and your child:
  — "I really like the way you pick up and carry the puppy so carefully!"
  — "Thanks for being so quiet while I was talking to Nana on the phone. Now, what was it that you wanted to tell me? I'm all ears."
  — "After I told you that you'd had enough cookies, you didn't ask me again. I really like the way you listen carefully even when you're not thrilled with what I have to

> say. I respect the way you do that and I'll bet lots of other people do also."

Exceptional parents know that such nonviolent approaches to correction help their child build confidence, frustration tolerance and resilience. Nonviolent approaches do this without imposing shame or reinforcing the violence found all around us. Exceptional parents, together with their extended family members, friends, and communities, create experiences for children that teach an alternative pattern. Through their own example when managing conflict with other adults and through their responses to their child's behavior, they help the next generation learn constructive, nonviolent, ways of managing their lives and relationships.

Key points:
1. Exceptional parents make every touch to another human being a loving touch.
2. Remember that young children don't *misbehave* as much as we may assume. Instead, they behave in ways consistent with their stage of development and it's our job as parents to help them learn.
3. Violence (slapping, spanking, beating) doesn't teach anything constructive. Instead, it teaches fear, distrust, resentment, self-loathing and the perpetuation of violence in order to gain power for oneself later on.
4. While violent choices may come to mind first because we so often see violent responses to conflict, there are many nonviolent choices that teach children positive behavior and values.

Appreciating Differences
Pink, the popular singer-songwriter, wrote a song called *RaiseYour Glass* that celebrates people who are "wrong in all the right ways." Hearing it always brings a smile to my face. In one short phrase she refutes the absurdity of a *power over* world in which being

different, so often a hallmark of courage and creativity, gets tagged as wrong. I join her in heralding a new world, one in which every way of being human that does no harm to others is a right way. Here we can learn from our differences rather than fear them. We can rest assured that, while you, your child, and others may differ wildly from one another in some ways, we nevertheless share the same humanity. Exceptional parents embrace this world of caring and respect.

I share the next story with some apprehension because of the jarring impact it may have on some readers. After thinking it over, however, I decided that what the story shows us outweighs any potential discomfort. I reminded myself that some of the most important things I've learned have resulted from confrontations with disturbing truths about human beings, including disturbing truths about me. So here goes.

A friend of mine shared this tale with me. She recalled standing third in line for checkout at her local grocery store. She, like many others present, was charmed by the lively banter between the cashier and her customer's baby daughter. The little white girl seated in the shopping cart was probably no more than 18 months old. She played peek-a-boo and chattered happily with the cashier, a dark-skinned black woman. After her mother paid and said goodbye to the woman behind the register, the little girl waved and cried out, "Bye-bye, monkey!" Her mother, according to my friend, looked mortified. She sputtered words of apology to the cashier, whose expression now suggested confusion tinged with disgust. The cashier composed herself with a shrug, then smiled graciously at mother and child as they made their exit.

Now, lest this story confuse you—possibly because some parents use "little monkey" and other such nicknames as terms of endearment for their children—please note that depicting African-Americans as monkeys (subhuman, in other words) in both words and images is one of the earliest and most enduring racist assaults. (You may be interested to know that an African-American friend advised me to add this clarification so every reader would understand the negative implications of what the child said. A white colleague, on the other hand, advised me that the clarification was unnecessary.)

Knowing that people come in many hues, genders, sexual orientations, faiths, ethnicities and backgrounds, exceptional parents do all they can to convey this to their child, helping her or him recognize individuals across this rich diversity as members of our same human family. Hopefully, the mother in the story mentioned above corrected her child by letting her know that the cashier was a person and that people have lots of different skin colors.

Given the ongoing separation of our communities along race and class lines in many places across the United States, and the sheer isolation of many families—with large numbers of people connecting mostly through technology—meaningful person-to-person interaction has become increasingly rare. While we may lament the loss of the deep connections that are only possible when people visit face-to-face, the advent of modern technology also offers opportunities for exposure to people different from ourselves. Through whichever means we encounter one another, whether in person or through the magic of computers, the conversations we have about our differences determine the meaning of those differences. Some suggestions for constructively shaping such conversations with children follow:

- Identify obvious differences and invite your child to do the same. Pretending color blindness and blindness to other differences does not help your child. Instead, a parent's denial of reality only adds confusion. (Denying reality rarely benefits children, or adults for that matter.) In truth, each of us with eyesight sees differences in skin color, gender, hairstyle, clothing and many other human attributes.
- Speak positively about differences. This habit affirms *power with* and directly challenges *power over*. After visiting with a diverse group of friends or watching a video that features

people with many different skin colors, ask your child to identify the differences that he or she noticed. Talk about the fact that human beings come with many different skin colors, all of them special and beautiful. Describe the historical points of origin across the world for people of many colors: black people originating in Africa, red/brown skinned people in North and South America, white people in Eurasia and yellow skinned people in Asia.

* Describe racism in age-relevant terms. Even small children can understand that differences in skin color are used as a reason to bully and steal from some people. Ask your child if they've ever seen another child treated badly because they're different. Talk about the history of conquest, slavery and inequality that has been justified and fueled by racism. Describe how this history continues to persist today, challenging each of us to work toward ending thinking and behavior that gives greater value and privilege to people with white skin while endangering people with skin colors other than white.

* In a similar fashion, encourage your child to notice different genders and sexual orientations. Help them notice, for example, that not all people fall neatly into two categories, male and female. Introduce your child to the reality that transgendered people expand gender into a complex and beautiful set of possibilities. Similarly, help your child identify gay, lesbian and bisexual people by pointing out the couples and families these individuals form, noting that all the possibilities for gender and sexual orientation are equally special. Even small children can understand that some men fall in love with women and others fall in love with other men, with the same being true for women.

* Talking about gender, you can also describe the history of men treating women as less valuable than themselves and heterosexual people doing the same thing to people who are not

heterosexual, sexism and heterosexism/homophobia respectively. Ask your child if they've ever heard "You run like a girl!" or "That's gay!" while they're at school. You may also talk about transphobia— the ways that many societies have traditionally punished and excluded transgender people. This stands in contrast to the long history within many tribal societies in the Americas, as well as in many other places across the world, of valuing transgender people for their uniqueness. In some of these societies, a transgender person's specialness is thought to make them exceptionally insightful and wise, and even sacred in some cases.

• Invite your child into similar conversations about all the differences that form the mosaic of humanity. Point out that some people use a wheelchair or canes to help them move from one place to another, some people cannot hear or see and so sense the world differently, and some people live with illnesses or gifts of nature that make their physical, mental and emotional capabilities different from those who do not share their circumstances.

• Make the most of opportunities to help your child acknowledge human differences of all types, including height, hair color and texture, eye color, the varied ways that we laugh, our tendency to either jump into conversations and activities wholeheartedly or devote time to thinking first, speaking and acting more cautiously. Helping your child identify and value human differences visible and invisible, significant and less significant, will prepare them to connect positively with people of all sorts.

As I mentioned earlier, exceptional parents know that the importance of these "valuing differences" conversations resides in their challenge to the *power over* mindset that has made the world such a dangerous place for so many people. These conversations promote a vision of humanity based upon *power with,* the power of love.

Exceptional parents live their commitment to the principle of *power with* by nurturing real connections to people from backgrounds both similar to, and different from, their own. They also go beyond paying attention to the ways that they and people similar to them have been disadvantaged by history and current social realities to consider the ways they and people like them receive advantages, understanding that it is far easier to look up into the hierarchy of *power over* and feel righteous indignation about the way *people like me* have been oppressed than it is to look down the hierarchy and grasp how *people like me* have been privileged.

For me, this means recognizing the privileges that come with being white and male, and using these whenever possible to benefit people who do not receive the same privileges. When involved with hiring decisions at work, for example, I support the importance of building teams in which people from a variety of backgrounds fill leadership roles. Creating not only workplace circles but also friendship circles that include people from across the spectrum of differences brings each of us a rich tapestry of viewpoints and experiences.

For the youngest among us, the habits described here can nurture a growing understanding of the rich variety among people, and a solid understanding that, while we may look and behave in ways that vary greatly, we all still belong to the same family. There are no monkeys among us, only human beings.

Key points:
1. While our differences may be rich and varied, we are all members of the same human family.
2. Identify and positively value differences rather than pretending not to see them. Denying reality only creates confusion and helps no one, including children.

3. Bringing people of many different backgrounds into your family's circle of friends will enrich the lives of everyone involved.

4. We can rise to one of the key challenges of our time by paying attention to our privileges and working to create a world in which everyone shares them.

Chapter 3

Spiritual Habits

You are not separate from the whole ... You don't have a life.
You are life.
—Eckhart Tolle, spiritual teacher and author

Spirituality means different things to different people. For most of us, it means feeling connected to something greater than ourselves in ways that bring inspiration, gratitude, opportunities to help other people, and joy. Our spirituality affirms the preciousness of life, as well as our place of belonging in the world. It reinforces values like mutual respect, kindness and love for one another. Our children deserve all of this and, as always, we are their first teachers and role models. This chapter explores a variety of ways that we can help our children experience all that spirituality has to offer.

The way I see it, there are no right and wrong ways to practice spirituality as long as we cause no harm to others. Some of us find spirituality primarily through our religion. My husband loves his Congregationalist church. He enjoys the fellowship and service opportunities that his church provides. Religious and non-religious people alike also celebrate their spirituality through a variety of activities not specific to any particular faith. We can awaken our spirituality through participation in team and individual sports, volunteering, doing the work that provides our livelihood and participation in cultural events. I have heard friends describe an evening with the Lincoln Center's *Mostly Mozart Festival Orchestra* as a "spiritual high."

As I write these words, I recognize what I'm doing as yet another form of spiritual practice. I'm grateful for the opportunity that writing this book gives me to share with you my best thoughts on parenting. I give you this chapter hoping that it will help you help your children benefit from the spiritual aspect of life.

Finding Spiritual Connection

Many young people today feel spiritually adrift. Brad Harrington, executive director of the Boston College Center for Work & Family, recently gave a presentation confirming this to the Employee Assistance Roundtable, the professional association for leaders of employee assistance and behavioral health programs located inside corporations (programs such as mine) and other large employers, including universities, hospital systems, and federal, state and provincial governments. Brad shared research showing that the majority of business majors enrolled in undergraduate and graduate level degree programs here in the United States have little sense of their life's meaning and purpose. Students of the humanities scored somewhat higher in this regard but, because business majors outnumber all other majors in both undergraduate and graduate programs, the research suggests that a great many young people pursuing higher education feel lost spiritually.

I imagine you join me in finding this sad. Spirituality, after all, is a pillar of health and wellness. It contributes to overall wellbeing at least as much as the other pillars: physical, emotional, social, and financial. The key message here: Exceptional parents help their child adopt positive values, feel a deep sense of their life's value, develop a sense of purpose, and know they are part of something larger than themselves.

Helping our child gain these spiritual strengths, like so much else about parenting, may seem simple in concept but prove less simple in practice. The key lies in demonstrating our own positive beliefs and values over time and showing through our example how these strengths help us through the challenging times. As we know, our children pay close attention to what we do.

A personal statement that describes your beliefs about the value of your life, the meaning of existence, and your purpose for living can help chart your course, but what you say must line up with your actions. Here's some of my own "self-talk" about spirituality: I consider my life a gift from divinity that is both beyond my capacity to understand and, at the same time, everywhere in evidence—in the air we are so perfectly suited to breathe, in the water that sustains us, in the unfathomable beauty of nature. My life is a gift of immeasurable value. I feel deeply connected to the tangible world as well as the world beyond substance, the world of spirit. For the past two decades I have described the meaning and purpose of my life as follows: to use my voice, writing skills, and talents as a therapist to bring more safety, health, and joy to others, and thereby leave the world a better place for my son and the generations that follow. As I enter the later phase of my life—I'll turn 57 this year—my personal mission statement has expanded to include: I will do what I can to heal the living planet, the source and sustainer of everything I know and value, including human beings.

These statements not only help me connect my daily activities to their value, meaning, and larger purpose, they also help me navigate the challenges and changes that come my way. I chose to accept the job offer from Prudential 19 years ago because it gave me the opportunity to help a great many people while also providing a higher standard of living for my family. Now, as my son enters young adulthood and no longer needs my financial support, I can explore new options for connecting my spiritual purpose as a therapist and leadership consultant to the call I feel to devote more time and energy to healing the planet. My personal mission statement helps shape my choices, which in turn, help me to further refine and revise my mission statement.

I'll give you a very simple example of how positive spiritual role modeling can go awry. My husband Tim and I were on line to get tickets at TKTS, the discount ticket vendor located in the center of Times Square in New York City. Hundreds of people joined us there, making the line stretch a great distance. We'd been waiting for about 45 minutes and the selling booth was within sight when a woman, holding the hand of her elementary-school-aged daughter, strode alongside the line for a bit and then, after a brief exchange with the couple standing in front of us, stepped behind them. She had cut the line in front of Tim.

Startled, we both looked at her and then at each other. Tim moved into action. He told her in no uncertain terms that she would not be holding that place in line.

She looked at him and said, "I came all the way from New Jersey and this line is so long."

We also had traveled from our home in New Jersey. Many other people on line had undoubtedly made a similar or even longer journey. Tim fixed his eyes on her and said nothing. She got the message and stepped out of the line.

What stays with me from that experience is the look on the little girl's face as she heard these words exchanged. She looked down at the ground and then across the square as she held her mother's hand. I felt sad for her, imagining that she felt embarrassed by her mother's behavior. She probably wished herself miles away.

Moment to moment, we demonstrate our beliefs about our values, our sense of connection to the people and larger world around us, and the meaning we make of our lives. In the moment described above, a mother acted out her belief that personal convenience trumps courteous regard for others. While in the large scheme of things this mother committed a minute offense—she didn't steal or cause physical harm or even say anything hostile. Nonetheless, she left her child looking as though she wanted to be apart from their shared moment, a spiritual abandonment that may linger in the little girl's memory as it has in mine.

At those times when we live our higher values, however, we help our child grow in spiritual connection. A colleague and her husband, along with their two preteen children, spent the month of August a few years back in a southern New Jersey town hit hard by Hurricane Sandy. The family devoted their annual vacation to helping repair and rebuild homes. Through personal experience, this vacation taught their children the benefits that can be gained putting positive values —generosity, kindness and caring—into action.

I have friends who spend one or two evenings each month answering suicide prevention and intimate partner violence telephone support lines. While their teenaged children cannot directly participate in these activities, they know of their parents' efforts and ask many questions. Their vicarious involvement in mom and dad's volunteer work undoubtedly enriches them spiritually.

We demonstrate our spirituality through choices large and small made every day. Simple habits matter: choosing to dispose of our trash properly instead of littering, placing recyclables in the appropriate bin, and picking up after our dog when we take them for a walk. These show our positive regard for the world around us.

Sometimes we receive unexpected opportunities for generosity, a hallmark of spirituality. In 2013 my husband and I sold our home in Morristown, New Jersey, and moved to our new home in Palmer, Massachusetts. A week after the house in New Jersey came under contract for sale, two large limbs fell from a pair of trees that stand on the property line. Fearing that more debris may follow, I asked an arborist to take a look. He told me that no work was needed at present but at some future time the trees, which grew from a single base and were ultimately destined to fall as a result of this unstable arrangement, should either be chained together or removed. Not wanting to leave this problem behind me, I had the two large trees removed.

This was not lost on my son, who remarked on how good it felt to know that I gave our neighbors this parting gift.

Crafting a personal mission statement and using it as a guidepost for decision-making can help us live according to our values and the meaning that we make of our time here on earth. Of course, this is not a tool that holds value for everybody. Some people find their spiritual strength primarily through membership in a community of faith or other social network, deeply meaningful multigenerational cultural patterns and/or belonging to institutions of various types. These may be universities, professional associations, altruistic institutions such as Habitat for Humanity and The American Cancer Society, and even workplaces. Some people find spiritual connection and draw spiritual strength from their involvement in cultural events involving music, theater, and dance.

There are no correct and incorrect ways that human beings connect to that which is larger than us, construct positive values, and find meaning. For some people, spirituality means direct connection with the natural world. I'll explore this more in the next section. In whatever ways best fit for you, your attention to your own spiritual development provides an example that will almost certainly strengthen your child.

Key points:
1. Exceptional parents help their child adopt positive values, feel a sense of meaning and a constructive purpose in life, and know they are part of something larger than themselves.
2. They do this through consistent and positive role modeling of their own spirituality and helping their child identify how they, too, can connect meaningfully with something larger than themselves.
3. It helps some people to write a personal mission statement as a guidepost for decision-making when life presents significant challenges and opportunities.

Embracing Nature
Not long ago, human beings related to the natural world in a more hands-on way than most of us do in our current age of industrial farming, global transport, and Super Stop & Shop. Before the great expansion of expressways during the late 1940s and early 1950s in the United States, a development that enabled long-distance transport of food and other products, many families, not just farming families, tended gardens that gave them at least some of their food. They canned fruits and vegetables and stored apples and root crops in their cellars. Food not produced at home came from nearby: fresh produce in its season. Everyone knew that radishes, peas and strawberries come early and tomatoes, squash and apples much later. Hunting, fishing, berry picking and nutting were common activities.

Ken Dolan-Del Vecchio

It was typical to keep a flock of chickens for eggs and meat, and not unusual for families, even city-dwellers, to raise rabbits.

Elders lived their later years in the family home, receiving care from loved ones. After they died, their bodies were not typically removed by professionals and embalmed (the practice of embalming and the profession of undertaking did not emerge in the United States until the late 1800s). Instead, family members bathed, dressed and displayed their relative's body at home, inviting others to visit and pay their final respects before the deceased's funeral and burial. People knew death as a part of life rather than something fearsome or catastrophic.

By age 5 or 6, most children had participated in these family activities. Everybody—by necessity—was both aware of and, at least to some extent, connected to the cycles of the natural world. As a result, people knew they belonged to the larger story of life on Earth, and many drew spiritual strength from this knowledge.

Fast forward to today. Many people live so far removed from nature that they've lost this understanding, and, along with it, a source of spiritual nourishment. The key message here: Exceptional parents practice simple habits that help them stay connected to the natural world. They invite their child to do the same. Thus, they not only provide their child with ready access to a source of spiritual sustenance, they also teach them the importance of protecting the natural systems that support all of our lives. This second point bears special emphasis, for we parents will likely leave a degraded environment to those who follow. Doing all we can to avert such a future seems, at minimum, only fair. Better still, helping our child participate in efforts to restore the health of natural systems will prepare her or him for responsible adulthood in a challenging new world.

My son Erik, a philosophy major, recalls listening to a renowned professor lecture on nature and spirituality. The speaker described some of his adventures camping in the Adirondacks, hiking through Pacific Northwest forests, and tending his family's garden in suburban Virginia. He talked about how he reawakens the serenity found in these experiences by devoting just a few quiet moments to deep breathing, and how this works for him regardless of the surroundings in which he finds himself. He told his class: "Having spent so much time with my hands in the soil, my eyes on the forest canopy listening to running brooks and singing birds, and taking in the smells of earth and rain, I can revisit these experiences by simply allowing myself a few moments of quiet time."

Erik remembers a fellow student saying, "I believe in my head that everything is connected to everything else, which means of course that we're connected to nature, but exactly how we're connected confuses me." He paused, and then asked, "Can you help me grasp how I'm connected?"

The professor said, "You can experience the connection when you take a step back from your thoughts and instead allow yourself to become quietly present in the moment, paying attention to the aliveness within your own body."

Erik described how the professor then led his 200 or so students through 10 minutes of meditation. With eyes closed and guided by the professor's words delivered in a quiet, soothing tone, they sank into their seats and focused on relaxing their muscles, progressing slowly from their shoulders to their toes, all the while breathing deeply. Once totally relaxed, they visited in their mind's eye a natural scene of their choosing, perhaps the seashore at dawn or a woodland brook on a cool spring afternoon. The professor instructed them throughout the exercise to focus on their breathing and let their mind's chatter recede into the background.

After opening their eyes, a number of students mentioned how calm they felt during and after the experience. The young man whose question prompted the meditation understood for the first time the connection between deep breathing and the clean air of forest and seashore. "It also struck me in a new way that I'm made mostly of water—that the blood rushes through my heart and blood vessels like water rushing through streams," he said. "For the first time I feel like I *got* the connection between me and the rest of nature in an emotional way."

In a more solemn tone, the professor began to talk about the importance of valuing nature not only in the abstract, but in reality as well. "Going there through meditation benefits us, but actually being in nature brings a far deeper appreciation for the value of this connection," he told the class. "Being outdoors reminds us of who and what we are, feeding the spirit in ways that go beyond my ability to describe. There's a dead serious consideration here also. Nature doesn't just feed the spirit. Air, sunshine, soil, water and the work of our fellow earthlings in making food, cleaning the environment, and in other ways keeping Earth's living systems in balance, make it possible for us to live. If human beings don't begin to value nature more highly we will continue to destroy the natural world, and ultimately this means destroying ourselves as well."

I am thrilled that this man helps young people experience this aspect of spirituality and its implications for the future. As the good professor said, we can gain spiritual nourishment any time we allow ourselves to simply *be* and reflect on the aliveness within and its connection to the rest of creation. We don't even need to close our eyes and experience a guided meditation.

As parents, we can also practice simple, everyday activities that help us and our children feel enriched by our connection to nature. These include gardening (simply growing basil and oregano in a kitchen window qualifies), creating landscapes that bring wild birds close to our homes (those who live in small apartments can attach to a window a small bird feeder or nest box that comes with suction cup mounts). Expressing our connection to nature may also include composting, recycling, using non-toxic household cleaners, and working for causes that challenge environmental destruction and support restoration. I'm sure you can identify many more as well. I'm going to devote the final part of this conversation to something that's particularly close to my heart—caring for animal companions.

As I discussed in another book, *The Pet Loss Companion: Healing Advice from Family Therapists Who Lead Pet Loss Groups,* we can gain many spiritual rewards by bringing nature's ambassadors—animal companions—into our families. One such reward is more consistent grounding in the present moment. Animals live in the only moment any of us truly has. They never check their mobile phones to see who just called or texted, nor do they get preoccupied with worries about money and work that needs doing. They never give only half their attention because they're busy planning what's next. In their world, paraphrasing the words of Ekhart Tolle, no matter what the clock says, the time is always *now.*

Have you watched a child grow quiet while her eyes track the fish in a home aquarium or her hands gently stroke her guinea pig? Interacting with animal companions, getting in sync with them, allows us to settle into the *present.* They help us achieve a level of calm that not only soothes the spirit but also heals the body. Research has shown, for example, that petting a dog can lower blood pressure, elevate mood and lessen stress.

Companion animals can also teach us much about how to interact lovingly with others. Animals respond with complete honesty—no lies, betrayal, or manipulation. Kindness toward them is reflected in their behavior toward us. An enthusiastic hug provokes sloppy dog kisses; gentle scratches behind the ears increase the volume of a tabby's contented purring; the rhythmic application of curry and brush help earn the steady calm and closeness of a horse friend.

Caring for an animal also reconnects adults and children alike with nature's life cycle. Puppies, kittens, chicks and other baby animals require exceptionally gentle handling and forgiving attitudes, for all little ones make mistakes. Raising them to adulthood teaches volumes about tenderness, persistence and acceptance. As their lives draw to a close, animal companions share their final lessons with us.

All parents want to protect their children from pain, including emotional pain. Life, however, brings unavoidable losses, and having animal companions within our families helps both adults and children learn to accept the circle of love and grief—for grief is the inevitable cost of having loved.

Modern civilization separates us from closeness to the natural world, a closeness that can be a key source of spiritual healing and, also, the inspiration for efforts to restore the natural systems that we have so dangerously damaged. Exceptional parents recognize this reality. They practice habits that help their child connect with the natural world in a way that offers meaning and healing. In doing so, both parent and child gain spiritually.

Key points:
1. Exceptional parents practice simple habits that help them stay connected to the natural world. They invite their child to do the same.
2. Recognizing our place of belonging within the larger systems of life on Earth can bring feelings of awe, belonging and gratitude, the essence of spiritual healing.
3. Simply taking time to pay attention to the similarities between human beings, other animals and the larger forces of nature can bring awareness of our spiritual connection to the natural world.
4. Activities such as gardening, hiking, working to end environmental destruction, and caring for companion animals can enhance spiritual health.

Asking for Help
Asking for help ranks high on the list of healthy spiritual habits. It undoubtedly rivals gratitude for the number one position, and for good reason. When adults ask for help we demonstrate spiritual maturity: the awareness that we are part of something greater than any one individual will ever be and the willingness to

ask humbly for what we need instead of hanging onto the illusion that we can manage all of life's challenges alone. What we gain as a result goes beyond filling the specific need of the moment. When we ask for help, we grow bigger than our pride and fear. We make the perhaps surprising discovery that humility and vulnerability in the company of those we trust never weaken or diminish or humiliate us. On the contrary, we grow stronger as a result. We find this happens whether we ask a family member, friend, neighbor, helping professional, a deity of our faith, or the universe in its entirety.

In our *power over* world, asking for help does more than benefit us individually. Each time we help one another, we take a step toward building a new *power with* world. In this new world, the one we hope our children inherit, we offer more love and support to one another. We know community, something too rarely known today.

Exceptional parents lead the way. They seek help with everything from driving directions to computer skills to parenting to their own unhealthy behaviors. They reach out to others whenever doing so will benefit them and their loved ones. They put aside pangs of pride, fear, embarrassment and envy in favor of the wisdom and peace of mind and human connection that's available for the asking. They also wisely recognize that asking for help shows respect, offering others the opportunity to feel useful, something most of us value.

Most important of all, exceptional parents let their child know that they regularly ask for help. They tell their child stories about how they've gained from using this skill. And they encourage their child to seek help from his or her teachers, guidance counselors and other trusted adults. First and foremost, they encourage their child to come straight to their parents whenever they feel uncertain, confused and in need of guidance.

I have seen countless friends, neighbors, therapy clients, colleagues and community members seek help for matters across a continuum of severity. These include minor conflicts with coworkers, marital difficulties, intimate partner violence, post-trauma symptoms, addictions of many kinds, and mood and thinking disorders. Through seeking and receiving help, the vast majority of these people achieved positive change, healing and renewal of hope. I have had the privilege of leading therapy and support groups for people who've suffered the loss of a loved one, parents fostering challenging young people, and survivors of intimate partner violence. The help exchanged within these meetings has been nothing short of inspirational. None of the participants were ever diminished by seeking help. On the contrary, those who struggle through their challenging times with dogged isolation suffer most.

For many of us, asking for help and then following through with the guidance we receive does not come easily. It has certainly not been easy for me. Looking back, I see my study of psychology and social work and my professional training in family therapy spotlighting an uncomfortable truth: While I have always loved the opportunity to help others, as a young man I found it more comfortable learning how to help others than learning how to ask for the help I needed personally. Another way of saying this: One of the reasons I learned how to be a therapist was so that I could also learn how to help myself.

This strategy worked well because my post-graduate training required me to seek therapy to examine my own family history, identify important personal issues, and work to resolve them. This work helps therapists avoid unwittingly inflicting their own unresolved issues upon their clients. After this training experience, I grew far more comfortable with asking for help when I need it— from friends, family members, colleagues, therapists and others. I wish I had acquired this skill earlier.

Let me share an example of what I meant when I mentioned how a therapist may unwittingly inflict their own issues on their client, for there is an important caveat here. Many years ago, shortly after I graduated from college, a therapist advised a friend of mine to sever her friendship with another friend rather than confront their relatively minor disagreement and try to resolve it. Against my advice and the advice of others, my friend followed the therapist's recommendation. This brought great pain to both of my friends, costing them each a valuable relationship. Decades later, each still talks sadly of this ending and the fact that they never reconciled.

Looking back, I see the therapist's recommendation as a mistake that probably stemmed from her own family history of disconnecting from people instead of facing conflict. Had she addressed this in her own therapy, I'm convinced she would have coached my friend to constructively confront our other friend rather than discard such a valued bond.

Here's the caveat: While asking for help opens us to a world of good advice, it also invites bad advice as well. Good judgment, yours and that of your most trusted friends and family members, can help you recognize the difference. It never hurts to discuss the advice you've received with the wise and loving people who know you well, perhaps including your spouse, parents, best friends or community of faith leader.

As my friends' experience those many years ago shows, bad advice can come from highly credentialed professionals, including those who make their living providing guidance. Never forget that degrees of professional competence vary. This holds true for therapists, psychiatrists, physicians, counselors, clergy, professors, teachers, plumbers, masons and other service contractors. Some perform brilliantly, most perform adequately, and a few perform dismally. You owe it to yourself to choose professional helpers carefully, apply your own judgment to their recommendations, and talk over their guidance with trusted others as well. Similarly, it's important to encourage your children to share with you the advice they receive from teachers, guidance counselors and peers so that you can help them evaluate it. Most professionals whose work involves caring for or teaching children provide helpful guidance. It can never hurt, however, for your child to share the advice they've received with you.

Having spent more than two decades now as a family therapist, health and wellness executive responsible for a team of therapists, and educator of behavioral health professionals, I feel the need to give a few more pieces of advice here.

When seeking a therapist, start with referrals from people you trust. Consider scheduling interviews with two or more therapists before committing to a series of meetings with any one of them. Ask them about their experiences helping people with concerns similar to yours. Ask them to describe their overall approach to helping. *Ask whatever questions you'd like answered about their professional background and the services they provide.* The professional you choose will expect you to share extraordinarily personal matters with them. It's only reasonable that they share freely with you the details of their professional background and approach to helping. Finally, because research shows that the quality of the relationship between a therapy client and his or her therapist best predicts the effectiveness of their work together, it makes sense to pay special attention to the way you feel toward those you interview. The importance of interviewing before committing to becoming a client applies also when seeking other kinds of professionals, such as physicians, realtors, financial advisors, personal trainers and coaches.

Most of the time, of course, we're not asking a professional for help; we're asking a family member, neighbor, friend, or coworker. As a reward, we not only get to share the other person's wisdom, we also boost our relationship with them. After all, asking for help shows respect for the person asked, bringing the two of you closer together.

When your child witnesses this happening, he or she learns valuable lessons: that we are wiser together than we'll ever be alone, that sharing advice brings families, friends, and communities together, and that we demonstrate and gain strength when we ask for what we need. There will be many times when your child will benefit from seeking guidance from teachers, coaches, friends, and, perhaps most importantly, you. Demonstrating your own willingness to seek help when you need it provides powerful encouragement for your child to show the same kind of strength.

Key points:
1. Asking for help and following through when we receive sound guidance is an essential life skill that demonstrates wisdom and strength.
2. It never hurts to discuss the advice we receive with trusted friends and family members before taking action.
3. It pays to choose a helping professional with care and never hurts to interview more than one in order to decide who will best meet your needs.
4. When a child sees a parent benefiting from asking for and receiving help, they become more likely to practice this skill themselves.

Cultivating Joy

Do you know people so full of joy that you can't help but smile when you think of them? If you're not one yourself (and I'm not, personally), you may see these individuals as anomalies, strangely gifted with exuberance or, for the more cynical among us, duped by *denial* of life's unpleasant realities. Many hours facilitating stress and change management programs for work groups, reading literature on positive psychology, and working alongside such radiant individuals has helped me to better understand joy.

I've learned that extraordinarily joyful people don't have some genetic difference that puts a permanent smile on their faces. Instead, they cultivate joy through a set of personal habits. Importantly, each of us can do the same: We can cultivate joy in the same way that we cultivate physical fitness and financial security—through the practice of daily habits. And we can encourage our child to do the same.

The key message here: Learning the habits that create joy can benefit each of us and our children as well. There can be few habits more important to cultivate as we strive to become exceptional parents. After all, isn't helping our child lead a joyful life one of our highest priorities?

What are these habits? We'll visit with one of those extraordinarily exuberant individuals to see him in action, but first I'd like to share an observation. Working as both a family therapist and organizational consultant, I have noted the parallels between the habits of exceptional parents and exceptional organizational leaders. Both depend upon the individual's awareness that they serve as an important authority figure, role model and protector for their family and team members respectively.

To be sure, many significant differences distinguish the two roles, but the cross-reference has value. I share examples from organizational life in this book on parenting because doing so emphasizes that parenting *is* leadership, and arguably the most important kind of leadership. Also, I do it because I've found that new information sometimes becomes easier to grasp when illustrated by a story a bit removed from the main topic. Finally, some readers undoubtedly fill the role of organizational leader in addition to parent. Emphasizing the connection between exceptional parenting and exceptional leadership outside the family may reinforce the best habits in both roles.

This past winter I received an invitation to give a talk for a business group with which I was not familiar. Roy Freiman, the group's leader, had requested an overview of my team's services. I arrived at his "town hall" meeting early to get a feel for the group and setting. As Roy and I said hello in person for the first time, he ushered me to a table that held carafes of hot chocolate. It was the middle of February, a time when the Northeast was trudging through one of our most severe winters on record. I mentioned that hot chocolate was a rare treat, something I'd never seen before at a business meeting.

Roy smiled broadly. "I know—it's different, and I thought it would put a smile on people's faces." *Joyful people make a habit of thinking of others and doing things likely to make them happy.*

Thus began one of the most pleasant hours I've experienced at work. The first 20 minutes belonged to Roy. With 50 or so of his staff in the room and another contingent dialing in via teleconference, Roy launched the meeting by congratulating two longtime team members on their anniversary dates. Noting that one of those being honored was a collector of sports statistics and the other a devotee of the silver screen, Roy had prepared questions on these subjects. First, he quizzed us on sports records set at milestone dates during the sports fan's 20 years of service. Next, he turned to the subject of the Academy Awards.

The honorees beamed during these quizzes. Each question provoked a round of unlikely guesses, including some intentionally ridiculous outbursts, after which the honoree deftly offered the correct response. Roy bestowed upon each a certificate of achievement before leading the group in raucous applause.

The tone shifted toward concern as Roy shared unfortunate news from a team member not in attendance. She had learned that her cancer, five years in remission, was active again. Roy told the group that she wanted them to know about the return of her illness, anticipating that their prayers, best wishes, calls and cards would boost her resolve as she underwent another round of treatment. Roy demonstrated great caring here as well as another habit of joyful people: He acknowledged a painful reality while also focusing on hope and the power of loving support.

Joy doesn't require denial. Quite the contrary, joyful people stay in the present moment, acknowledging even very painful truths, and they amplify reasons to be grateful and hopeful.

Next on the agenda: my introduction. By now I knew that Roy cared about the people around him. He took time to learn what interested them and he cared about their welfare. I didn't expect, however, that he'd taken time to learn something about me as well.

"Ken is an interesting guy," Roy began. "He works here in Newark, but he's got a whole bunch of animals at his place somewhere out in God's country, Massachusetts I think. He's got three little—well, I guess you can call them dogs but that may be a stretch. They're Chihuahuas, I believe. Am I right, Ken?"

I smiled and nodded.

"But that's not where it ends. Ken also has chickens and rabbits," Roy said in a tone suggesting bemused puzzlement. Then, after a moment's pause: "I think I'll leave it at that."

The group laughed.

"Oh yes, and Ken leads the Behavioral Health Services team here. He's here to talk with us about the services his organization provides. Let's give him a big welcome!"

The group applauded wildly.

I took advantage of Roy's introduction. "Yes, I have two tiny little Chihuahuas named Isabel and Abigail who are less than 6 pounds each, and one much larger Chihuahua named Jack," I said. "Also three chickens—each of whom has a name and is a beloved pet—and finally, two enormous rabbits who I similarly cherish. I make no apologies for my eccentricity. If I leave you with no other thought today than this one I will have done my job: *Indulge your eccentricities as long as they cause no harm to others, because they will likely bring you great joy.*"

My introductory remarks were followed by a lively discussion, and since that day I've had the privilege of working with Roy many times. Over coffee in the company's cafeteria one morning he said, "Look at the people coming and going from here. Too many of them look unhappy. We have to change that." As a result, he and I worked together to bring my team's seven-session "Choose Happiness" program to his group. They are now considering providing it, along with other health and wellness programs, to the company's life insurance customers as well. Roy is all about joy.

I've met people similar to Roy, but not many. As I mentioned earlier, his kind of attitude and the habits that bring joy seem to come readily to certain people, but the rest of us can learn to cultivate joy as well. The recipe calls for amplifying pleasant thoughts, memories and feelings. It emphasizes gratitude, caring about and giving to others, and practicing the skill of presence in the moment. These habits can help us more consistently experience joy. Just as important, teaching them to our children will empower them to bring more joy into their own lives.

One final observation: Some people, children among them, find that despite their best efforts, they cannot experience positive feelings with any consistency. Instead, they struggle much of the time with feeling sad, hopeless, apathetic, easily irritated, and empty, or some combination of these. No matter how hard they and their loved ones try to raise their spirits, these people may rarely experience even a hint of joy—or at best, brief flashes of happiness. As we'll discuss in more detail later, these individuals fall within the 10 percent of the U.S. population who live with clinical depression. Like diabetes and heart disease, clinical depression is a medical illness and a very serious one at that, for it can contribute to suicide. If you or your child suffers in the ways I've described above, please consult with a psychotherapist for an assessment. Both of you deserve the care that can greatly improve your frame of mind.

Key points:
1. Exceptional parents practice habits that bring them joy, encouraging their children to do the same.
2. These habits lie at the very center of the good things we offer our children because, beyond the basics of health and security, most parents' most precious wish for their child is a lifetime of joy.
3. Joyfulness flows from habits that include staying in the present moment, emphasizing gratitude, and giving to others.
4. Indulging our eccentricities—doing the things we find fun and interesting as long as we cause no harm—is another key habit for cultivating joy.
5. Exceptional parenting, the quintessential and most important family leadership role, shares many qualities with exceptional organizational leadership.

6. Adults and children who rarely experience even fleeting moments of joy deserve an evaluation for clinical depression, a serious illness for which highly effective help is available.

Being a Friend

Life is a team sport and having even one or two good friends on our team boosts us in countless ways. Friends give us our first experience of loving connection outside our families. Showing us the goodness in the world, genuine friends confirm our spiritual impulse to reach beyond ourselves with kindness and hope. Friends share love, support, acceptance, understanding, positive challenges, constructive criticism, a variety of perspectives and endless inspiration. Friends buoy one another through turbulent times, giving nurturance that, for the fortunate, will last a lifetime. Bearing witness to one another's lives across the years, friends become the coauthors of our shared life stories, helping us remember, make sense of, and cherish our time here.

Exceptional parents know that among the most important skills they can help their child develop are those that will help them make and keep friends. While these skills may come intuitively to some, let's review them so they stay close at hand.

- **Listening.** All relationships require listening, which is different from simply hearing. The difference: focused, respectful attention to the words another person speaks and the emotions that accompany them. When listening, we don't interrupt and instead strive to grasp as fully as possible that person's experience and meaning. When a friend tells us they feel happy, frightened or ashamed, we hear their words and inside ourselves call up the feelings they've mentioned. We show empathy by reflecting to our friend our sense of what they mean and how it feels for them: "You sound absolutely thrilled and I'm thrilled for you!" or "Wow, that sure does sound scary" or "I can see how badly you feel about this."

After listening carefully, we may ask for more details so we can gain an even deeper understanding of their experience.

- **Showing sincere interest over time.** Friendships begin when two people show a real interest in one another by listening carefully and empathizing with each other's experience. Friendships endure only when this interest and empathy continue over time. Our mutual interest becomes evident through back-and-forth dialogue about something meaningful. Children sometimes begin friendships when coloring, playing games or simply visiting in one another's homes. Each shows interest in something that's meaningful to the other. "I like the colors you're using" or "you're good at throwing the ball" or "you have such a fun doggie," they'll say to one another. Later on and into adulthood, friends ask questions about one another's likes and dislikes, schoolwork, family members, intimate partnerships, children, and work lives; and they remember what's been shared. One of the key ways our friendly interest in another person becomes known to them is when we recall things they have told us about their preferences, interests, life events and the important people in their lives.

- **Taking turns.** The most satisfying friendships feel balanced. So, in the description above, speaker and listener alternate roles. There come times when one friend needs to be listened to at length, and other times when that friend will be called upon to listen for an extended period. Similarly, there are times when one friend needs help and the other stands ready to assist, or when one friend's achievements warrant acclaim and the other enthusiastically plans the celebration. Friends embrace one another in ways in which goodness flows in both directions.

- **Spending time together.** Getting to know another person requires time spent in their company. Some people believe that friendships can take place entirely through electronic communication. My clinical experience with families, my own parenting experience, and stories from friends who have children has convinced me otherwise. We can trade information online but friendship requires something more. Friendship requires being in one another's presence, particularly during the early stages when getting acquainted, so that we can hear one another's words while seeing facial expressions and body language. Skyping, Facetime chats, and other face-to-face electronic experiences come close, but simply don't offer all that's needed in the beginning of a relationship. Many exceptional parents have a rule: they don't count anyone as a personal friend who they have not met in person. They also require their children to make online contact only with people with whom they also have in-person contact. I applaud such wisdom.

- **Accepting differences.** While friends often find one another through shared activities—they may have met playing field hockey or working on a project together—they don't expect one another to share identical interests and attitudes. One of my colleagues recently lost her best friend to congestive obstructive pulmonary disease (COPD). The two had known one another for more than 40 years. As my friend reminisced, she said, "Nora and I couldn't have been more different when it came to politics, but we just agreed to disagree and it never got in the way of our friendship." She went on: "We had the most wonderful times together and we'd do anything for one another. She gave me a plaque that I keep in my kitchen. It reads 'We've been through a lot together—and most of it was your fault.' I'll miss her for the rest of my days."

  Friends may argue with one another about their different ideas regarding even highly-charged subjects like politics, religion, and personal values, but they don't base their friendship upon trying to convince the other or reaching agreement. Instead, their friendship remains firmly grounded in their deep regard for one another, something far more important than their differences.

- **Recognizing personal boundaries.** The respect friends demonstrate for one another's personal boundaries is a key factor in their ability to weather important differences. Friends know that, while they may choose to share many personal details of their lives with one another, each will prefer to keep some matters private. Respecting privacy by never badgering the other person for more information than comfort dictates, friends show respect for one another's personal boundaries.

- **Demonstrating love.** All of the above contribute to the most important aspect of friendship, love. Friends show love for one another by doing all that's been described above. Note well that love describes a feeling, but the feeling we hold inside becomes evident to others only through our actions. Thus, friends do things for one another that cause the recipient to feel cared for, respected and treated with great consideration. Friends show love to one another by holding in confidence personal information rather than using it as fodder for gossip. Friends show their love by respectfully challenging one another when they feel a poor choice has been, or is about to be, made. They do this with tact and kindness, knowing that to avoid challenging their friend would be easier but less loving. Friends show their love by showing up in one another's lives during celebratory times as well as challenging times, providing unflagging encouragement, demonstrating trustworthiness and helping one another in every way possible.

Ken Dolan-Del Vecchio

As you may have noticed, many of the habits that I've described as hallmarks of friendship also describe the behavior of exceptional parents toward their child, the most important difference being the authoritative status that parents assume. (Within friendships, of course, there is a balance in which neither friend assumes the position of greater authority.) In most respects, then, exceptional parents model the basics of friendship as they provide loving care for their child. They also demonstrate how loving friendships operate whenever their child witnesses, or hears stories about, their parent's own friendships.

My friends, Maryam and Marie, met in their postgraduate family therapy program nearly 25 years ago and have been best friends ever since. Maryam has three teenage daughters. Marie has a young adult son and daughter. I met Maryam and Marie at the same time as they met one another. We were students together. While I've stayed in touch and get together with them periodically, I live at a distance and don't have the depth of friendship with them that they enjoy with each other. Nevertheless, I've participated in many gatherings throughout the years that included Maryam, Marie and one or more of their children.

These two women so obviously enjoy one another that I can't help but smile as I write this. They hang on each other's words and tell raucously funny stories about the misadventures they've endured working together as therapists, at meditation retreats, and during weekend travels. They never fail to make everyone around them laugh to the point of tears, including their children, who they regularly invite into their conversations. Nobody could spend time with Marie and Maryam without witnessing the joy that comes from their friendship and learning something about how to be a friend. I am certain that their relationship serves as a model for their children as they shape their own friendships.

I want to close this discussion on friendship by pointing out something important (and also perhaps a bit frightening). As our child moves through their formative years, we continue to model the basics of friendship and our relationship with our child retains that important difference mentioned earlier—we remain the authority in the relationship. As our child enters adulthood, however, that dynamic begins to shift. Our child will likely become an authority in his or her own right, perhaps in a particular field of study, trade or profession. More important, he or she will become the authority over his or her own life. As this shift happens, exceptional parents relinquish their earlier authority over their child, becoming more of a friend in every sense.

We will always remain our child's parent, holding our special status as a first role model. Almost certainly, there will remain details of our private lives that we will never wish to share with our child—nor would our child want to hear them. (Marsha, a colleague, told me that Sandra, her 31-year-old daughter, told her, in a joking tone but at the same time seriously, "I'd like to know about 80 percent of my Mom!")

The wisest among us, however, will relinquish our role of authority in our adult child's life in favor of something that becomes ever more akin to friendship. The most fortunate among us will one day joyfully note that our once-dependent child has indeed become a full-fledged adult, and one of our very best friends.

Key points:

1. Exceptional parents know the value of helping their child develop the skills that create and sustain friendship. They make every effort to teach these skills and also demonstrate them in their behavior toward their child and within their own friendships.

2. These skills include listening without interruption, showing sincere interest over time, taking turns, spending time together, accepting differences, respecting personal boundaries and demonstrating love.

3. The big difference between friendship and parenting is that parents take an authoritative role in the relationship during the years prior to adulthood.

4. Eventually, as our child becomes an adult, she or he will become the authority in her or his own life.
5. While you will always hold the special status of primary role model for your adult child and will likely never want to discuss certain aspects of your life with your adult child, you may ultimately be able to count him or her among your very best friends.

Excelling at Work

We expect schoolchildren to pay attention, learn new tasks, contribute their ideas, collaborate on shared projects, and treat others with civility and respect. The same expectations apply to most of us within our workplaces, making it apt to describe school as our child's first encounter with work. While he or she learns about schoolwork, our child also learns about the broader meaning, purpose and value of work by witnessing how we do ours and talking with us about this important area of life. Later, as our son or daughter matures toward adulthood and crosses the threshold into paid employment, our coaching and role modeling become even more important, for the world of work presents many challenges.

In addition to the practicalities of learning and providing income, work, ideally, also fills a spiritual need. At school, our child strives toward academic goals that bring them closer to fulfilling their potential for learning. He or she also develops artistic abilities and builds friendships. The work of adults—as a family therapist, homemaker, barista, sanitation worker, farmer or one of the myriad other vocations—provides service to others. Striving to learn, develop our creativity, and build loving connections with others, the work of schoolchildren (and, hopefully, the rest of us), and delivering service to others are spiritual endeavors.

This spiritual dimension of work—a potential source of personal fulfillment and positive energy—can get lost, however, when we don't feel good about what we're doing. Many people experience what they do for a living as grinding drudgery. In fact, a Gallup study published in the August 2014 edition of *Success Magazine* found that only 30 percent of the workforce feels "engaged and inspired," while the remaining 70 percent feels either "not engaged" or "actively disengaged." Translation: most people hate their jobs.

Knowing that our children pay close attention to us as role models, exceptional parents do their best to make their way into that fortunate 30%. It should be simple, right? Just learn to feel good about your job. Hardly so, I'm afraid. 70% of us wouldn't loathe what we do for a living if we could *easily* turn that around.

Particular habits, however, practiced over the long term can help us gain greater personal satisfaction from our work and move closer toward joining that fortunate 30% if we're not already among them. Years of observation, consultation with happy and unhappy entry-level to boardroom-level employees, as well as studying human behavior in the workplace, have helped me identify these habits. I've distilled them to an essential three: *Striving to develop extraordinary competence, assertiveness and kindness.* The more we practice these habits, talk about them, and coach our child to develop them, the more we parents and our children benefit.

Competence means demonstrating the skills, knowledge and ability to do your work effectively. Extraordinary competence means you take this a step further, committing yourself to doing your work exceptionally well. It helps greatly, of course, if you find your work interesting and gratifying. Let's say you studied or trained extensively—perhaps to work as a teacher, physician, plumber, or electrician—and once you began employment found the job to be all you dreamed it would be. Your passion will make it easier to develop and maintain extraordinary competence. You likely feel moved to do what's necessary to keep up-to-date with what's new in your field, perhaps even personally contributing scholarship on the most effective practices.

However, if circumstances compelled you to take a job, any job, to support yourself and your family—a reality for many people—you may find yourself in a more difficult situation. Here, it can help to identify two key aspects of your work: the *parts that you do find gratifying* and the *skills you're learning* that will help you find a job that suits you better. John, a friend's 22-year-old son, is learning to become an auto mechanic. He loves knowing that he's helping customers and learning more every day about engine repair. These positives currently outweigh the fact that John's boss rarely says a word of thanks and treats all the mechanics gruffly. Like this young man, if you hold those aspects of your job that you enjoy in the front of your mind, you may feel better as a result. You may also feel motivated to build the skills that will become your ticket out. Both of these can make the present moment a more positive one.

We can use our experiences on the job to help our child. If we love our work, we can talk with our child about how it adds to our life. We can help them identify the subjects at school that inspire their own interest (and perhaps even passion). If our child finds some or much of their schoolwork to be drudgery, we can help them identify the pieces that hold some interest and encourage them to emphasize these.

This may be as simple as encouraging your child to focus on their favorite subjects, emphasizing their joy in learning what these classes have to offer while recognizing their other subjects as tasks that simply need to get done. You may point out the parts of your job that you love, perhaps the feeling you get after helping to solve another person's problem, versus other parts that you find mind-numbing, such as filling out paperwork. You might explain that doing the boring work keeps your organization running, which allows you to do the rewarding work. I have a colleague who says he loves 50 percent of his job so much that it makes up for the 50 percent that's "administrivia."

In an even broader sense, sharing your realistic perspective on work can help your child understand that life sometimes feels a bit like a balancing act, one in which we get joy from some activities and must challenge ourselves to find the value within the other unpleasant but necessary ones.

Assertiveness, the second essential habit of those who excel at work, means recognizing your own needs and striving to meet them. This often requires speaking up about what you need from others. Because many people confuse assertiveness with aggression, I'll highlight some important differences between the two and then give examples:

- Assertiveness delivers and invites mutual respect. Aggression delivers and invites hostility.
- Assertiveness holds positive intentions. Aggression often seeks to hurt, take from, or diminish others.
- Assertiveness seeks personal empowerment but not at the expense of others. It fits in a *power with* world. Aggression tries to overpower others. It fits in a *power over* world.
- Assertiveness relies upon looking within oneself to identify one's own needs, sufficient self-respect to value them, and the courage to work toward meeting them. Assertiveness balances this effort by recognizing the needs of others and valuing those also. Aggression tries to satisfy one's own needs while disregarding the needs of others.
- Assertiveness seeks mutual understanding and mutual success. Aggression seeks to win.
- Assertiveness strives for fairness. Aggression strives for dominance.

Some examples of extraordinary assertiveness and competence:
- An employer's policy defines work hours as 9 a.m. to 5 p.m. Many managers and their teams, however, almost always work from 8 a.m. to 6 p.m. Kelly delivers extraordinary work and never strays from the 9 a.m. to 5 p.m. routine. Every day, she says a cheerful goodbye to her supervisor and coworkers on her way out the door at 5 p.m.. (Assertiveness is demonstrated here by actions rather than words.)

Ken Dolan-Del Vecchio

- Jamilla, a workplace leader, hears a new team member shouting obscenities over the phone. Jamilla wastes no time in asking her team member to join her in a private conference room. She informs the newcomer that she expects everybody on her team to address one another at a conversational volume and to use civil language, and that this goes for phone calls originating in the office as well. Jamilla explains that further outbursts will result in formal corrective measures, potentially as significant as termination of employment. In the days and weeks that follow, Jamilla makes a point of praising her new team member periodically when she "catches her" interacting professionally with others: "Given what we talked about with the sales team in that last meeting, I think we all may have felt frustrated; I like the way you kept your cool and stayed absolutely calm when you asked questions and gave answers."

- Phillip excels at his job and receives solid rewards and recognition. He knows, however, that employers frequently change course or are bought by other companies, both of which make continued employment uncertain even for stellar contributors. Consequently, Phillip knows that in addition to his everyday job, he also has the job of planning his career. He keeps his resume current, pursues continuing education to build knowledge and skills, stays in contact with a wide network of colleagues, and takes note of interesting job postings. He has a vision of the work he wants to be doing several years into the future and shapes his work-related activities as much as possible with this vision in mind.

- Despite delivering exceptional work, including contributing ideas leading directly to the results that distinguish their group's performance, Jameson never receives due credit. Instead, his boss has convinced higher-ups that he—the boss—deserves all the credit for the team's success. After confronting his boss about this several times and getting in return comments like, "I just didn't think to mention you, don't be so sensitive," Jameson changes his strategy. He continues to do his job with exceptional competence, but also starts putting a great deal of energy into a search for new employment. When competence and assertiveness meet with such unyielding disrespect, he knows it's time to look for a different job.

Most of us talk about our work when we're at home—after all, it's how we spend most of our time. My friends, Lynda and Pieter, have two young adult daughters, Jan and Sigrid. Lynda works as an independent human resources consultant and Pieter works within a large financial services company. These parents have long shared with their children stories about the importance of giving work "your all," standing up for yourself, seeking new and better jobs, and, in Lynda's case, courageously striking out on your own.

Jan and Sigrid have taken these stories and their parents' examples to heart. Jan, a superb writer, has contracts with a variety of business websites. When one of these websites slashed their per-word payment to contracted writers in half, Jan informed them that she would "of course" spend only half as much time writing their pieces and "the difference in quality will likely become noticeable as a result." She kept to her word and found new, higher-paying customers to fill her open time. Sigrid has shown similar gumption in her work as a veterinary technician. Noting that she loves caring for animals more than the other aspects of her job, Sigrid's saving her money with the goal of eventually starting a pet boarding business. She's also training as a groomer and taking courses in animal nutrition thinking that knowledge and skills in these areas will add to her earning capacity as well as her business' overall appeal.

Lynda and Pieter's example shows how extraordinary competence and extraordinary assertiveness can combine to help exceptional parents and, eventually, their children thrive and grow in their chosen careers. It pays to emphasize also that one of these attributes without the other can lead to trouble. Who among us has not witnessed an extraordinarily competent coworker who, lacking the confidence to assert himself or herself, gets passed over for pay raises, promotions, advanced training opportunities and rewarding assignments? On the other hand, how about coworkers who show great assertiveness but can't back it up with competence? Confidence without competence will eventually get unmasked as hollow bluster. I've heard this called "the impostor syndrome." Exceptional parents deliver both extraordinary competence and extraordinarily assertiveness—they walk the walk and they also talk the talk.

They also coach their child on assertiveness skills. They teach him or her the value of speaking one's mind in a respectful fashion, noting the many situations in which this applies. These include times when their child needs to better understand what a teacher or fellow student has said, when another child has said or done something hurtful, and at other times when they have a question or concern.

Kindness, another key ingredient for excellence at work, makes the exceptionally competent and assertive worker stand out from the rest of the top tier. Kindness wraps extraordinary competence and assertiveness in a shawl of compassion. Without it, the most competent and assertive among us risks creating unnecessary stress for ourselves and others who may work with us.

A decisive factor for excellence, kindness may also seem the simplest to carry out. Alas, experience tells a different story, for I have witnessed many people with brilliant technical skills and great assertiveness show disdain toward others.

Exceptional parents show that it needn't be this way. Michele led the sales division of a company 50,000 strong. A brilliant business strategist, she also treats everyone she encounters with kindness and humility—so much so that the mention of her name to almost anyone at the company where she worked evokes a smile and a story of how freely Michele gives thanks and credit to others, how willingly she assumes challenging responsibilities, and how compellingly she empowers others with her leadership skills. Michele and her partner have two young adult children who, at Michele's retirement event, spoke about how they've learned poise, humility, perseverance and service from their mom's example. Many who attended the event could identify with them, having learned so much the same from Michele personally.

Sheldon works in the produce department at a grocery store known for stocking organic and minimally processed foods. He excels at his job and stands up for his own needs and those of the people who work for him. The people who Sheldon supervises like him immensely. He's known to be exceptionally good at what he does and also exceptionally kind.

Sheldon has what amounts to a second full-time job caring for his developmentally-disabled son, 12-year-old Garrett. Like many parents of children with special needs, Sheldon has become a self-taught expert on his son's condition, options and resources for assistance, and the laws regarding school-based support. His extraordinary knowledge, assertiveness and diplomacy have resulted in Garrett receiving the comprehensive support he needs.

Other parents sometimes ask Sheldon how he's gathered all of these resources for his son, while they have repeatedly encountered stone walls and red tape. He believes that the answer lies in his competence in understanding his son's condition and related needs, his unrelentingly assertive advocacy, and his kind way of approaching others. Without the last of these, he feels certain his success would be lessened.

"Facing the challenges involved with getting all the right services in place can feel absolutely soul crushing," Sheldon says, "but I always remember that I'm talking with people who have feelings and stress in their lives, just like all of us. I talk with the people in these bureaucracies in a way that's persistent but also kind. I never lose sight of the fact that they have a tough job trying to manage so many families' requests."

Exceptional parents provide exceptional role modeling, including when it comes to work. They demonstrate extraordinary competence, assertiveness and kindness, and they gain personal gratification as a result. Their example, the workplace stories they tell, and the guidance they offer helps their child gain a similar reward during their school years and beyond.

Key points:
1. At heart, our work is spiritual practice, one of our most important gifts of service to others.
2. Exceptional parents strive to find satisfaction in their work, knowing that this brings personal rewards and, by example, will also help their child approach their own work with positive expectations.
3. When doing work in which we have little interest, it helps to recognize those aspects of the job that we *do* find gratifying as well as the skills and knowledge we're gaining that can help us find more fulfilling work.
4. Three important habits fuel great success in the world of work: extraordinary competence, assertiveness and kindness.
5. These three, practiced together, often contribute to workplace success. One or two without the third invites difficulties.
6. Most of us tell stories to our families about our work. We can use these stories to help our children learn how to approach their own work, first in the classroom and, later, in their careers.

Grit

At the heart of many people's spirituality lives a deep and abiding thankfulness for the gift of life. Such people often show their gratitude, at least in part, by striving to make the very most of their lives. They make persistent efforts to reach their fullest potential while also helping their loved ones and everyone else they touch do the same. Their determination remains undaunted even in the face of great obstacles, uncertainty, and setbacks. In a word, they show *grit*.

Exceptional parents fit this description. They follow their dreams, and in doing so, embolden their children to do the same. They enable a virtuous cycle in which their drive for fulfillment inspires their child to take on their own challenges with determination and optimism. We hear of such parents in stories like the one about a single mom who raised three children while struggling to make ends meet and, during her later years, worked tirelessly to improve neighborhood schools. We hear of the dad who passed up a major promotion to remain close with his wife and two sons—puzzling friends, his parents, and siblings, and contributing to loving family relationships and a cherished legacy of engaged fatherhood. We meet, or read about, parents who emigrated to the United States from a war-torn nation with no more than a few coins in their pockets and have managed to build a safe and loving home for their children as well as comfortable lives during their retirement years. While their challenges and goals vary, parents who strive for fulfillment, while also caring for their loved ones, give the next generation strength and an inspiring model for success.

If it takes grit to pursue our own dreams, it takes even more of it to let our child experience grit personally, for it requires allowing them to face their own difficulties without coming to the rescue. All of our parental instincts may rise in protest, but exceptional parents resist. They know that some things—learning to ride a bicycle and drive a car, knowing how it feels to fall in love, and trusting that you have grit—can only come from firsthand experience.

Exceptional parents know that adversity gives us the opportunity to build competence. They hold back on fixing situations their child can handle themselves. Instead, they stand ready to offer their thoughts and guidance if asked or if the child's age and developmental stage makes it essential for them to do so. This can mean

Ken Dolan-Del Vecchio

letting your child do their schoolwork without offering help that a more objective observer would call *doing it for them*. Instead, you may encourage them to seek help from their teacher by raising questions about the particular points that give them trouble. This simple redirection nurtures your child's growing ability to navigate the world beyond home, building in small steps an "I can do this!" attitude.

Let's say your child takes up a new sport, musical instrument or some other activity, finds the challenge more difficult than expected, and talks about quitting after the first couple of games or classes. You can help your child by encouraging him or her to persevere, teaching that building a skill requires sustained effort over time. Learning this important lesson—that competence grows through disciplined practice, and that this often feels uncomfortable in the beginning—will serve your child well throughout life.

Teaching grit, however, should never be confused with either forcing your child to go forward without appreciation for their likes and dislikes or abandoning them so they find themselves without the benefit of adult guidance. Instead, it requires providing the right amount of guidance and structure while also keeping enough distance that your child can take a developmentally reasonable level of personal responsibility. Careful judgment is the key element here. As in all matters, when faced with uncertainty parents owe it to themselves and their child to consult with other adults whom they trust and respect, sometimes including teachers, guidance counselors, school nurses, physicians and behavioral health professionals.

Children should *never* be expected to manage certain challenges alone. Bullying at school stands out as one example. Bullying—a pattern in which a person (or persons) with more power repeatedly and intentionally hurts another person who has less power—cannot be managed by the victim. A parent must contact school authorities on their child's behalf. Similarly, an adult must step in when a child faces any other kind of abuse.

As the years pass, we can allow our child an increasingly greater degree of personal responsibility, while continuing to voice encouragement and the reassurance that we're always happy to give advice when asked. For teens, this often means standing on the sidelines ready to provide coaching on friendship, dating, sex and substance use.

Ultimately, young people confront challenges regarding such issues as advanced education and training, employment, finances, marriage and the raising of their own children. At every stage, the more we allow our child to set their own course, make their own decisions, and learn from their mistakes, the better prepared they become for the challenges ahead.

Not long ago, a friend described a series of conversations that he and his wife had with their son, Greg, a college junior living on campus in a distant city. Greg phoned to report that he felt so bored with his part-time job "that I think I'm losing brain cells." His work involved phoning university alumni and parents of current students to solicit contributions to the university. Despite the boredom, he did good work that brought money to the university.

Greg had calculated that after quitting his job he'd be able to meet his expenses using savings from previous years' part-time and summer-time work. My friend told me that he and his wife, who their son contacted individually, gave him the same advice.

"We told him that the decision regarding whether or not to resign was his to make," my friend said. "We also told him that if he decided to resign it would be wise to do this in person and give at least two weeks' notice. We told Greg that a professional resigns in this way because the face-to-face approach conveys assertiveness and respect, while the two-week notice allows a bit of time to seek a replacement."

It turned out that Greg had planned to take an easier route. He'd expected to resign via email with no advance notice. He wasn't happy with his parents' advice because he, like most of us, didn't like the thought of facing his boss to deliver the news.

Grudgingly, Greg decided to follow his parents' advice. The result was enlightening. After listening to the young man's reasons for wanting to resign, his boss thought for a few moments and then shared an idea.

Noting boredom as the main problem, while also acknowledging Greg's success at soliciting donations, his boss proposed something more challenging. He offered the opportunity to work with the university's list of "high value" donors, those who sometimes gave substantial gifts. This offer piqued Greg's interest and he decided to stick with the job.

This story provides an example of how facing a challenge bravely—showing a bit of grit—can make a difference. Many of our children will face far greater challenges, such as addiction, unexpected pregnancy, significant loss and serious illness. When our child sees us approach our own lives—even the hard times—with optimism and determination, and experiences our faith in their ability to do the same, we have done our best to prepare them for whatever comes their way.

Key points:
1. Exceptional parents make persistent efforts to overcome the obstacles, uncertainties and setbacks that challenge the fulfillment of their potential. In a word, they show grit. They help their loved ones and everyone else who they touch do the same.
2. Resist the temptation to fix things that your child can resolve personally or with the help of their teachers, coaches or other trusted adults. Instead, help her or him gain competence by encouraging them to keep at it when the going gets rough, ask for and accept help, expect mistakes and learn from them.
3. Use careful judgment and the counsel of trusted advisors to decide whether or not it makes sense for you to take charge of an issue facing your child. Step in to help if your child faces bullying or any other kind of abuse.

Chapter 4
Healthy Habits

You're in pretty good shape for the shape that you're in.
—Dr. Seuss

Ken Dolan-Del Vecchio

When you've got your health, you've got just about every-thing you need! Wise indeed, this maxim reminds parents to do our best to equip our children with habits that promote lifelong wellness. We'll examine some of those habits in this chapter, ones related to physical health as well as others geared more toward emotional, behavioral, and financial wellness. All of these inter-weave—the physical, emotional, behavioral, and financial aspects of health—and each makes important contributions to our overall experience of well-being. The subjects of previous chapters, habits of heart and mind, people habits, and spiritual habits also make essential contributions to our well-being. They lay the foundation for overall health and our discussions about them will support the discussion we'll have in this chapter. Few topics have more impor-tance than this one, for when we help our children learn to take good care of themselves across all the dimensions of health they can go forward set to enjoy their best possible lives.

Minding the Basics of Health

While some things affecting physical health arrive as gifts of nature, such as a family history of high blood pressure, a grow-ing body of research confirms the importance of our daily habits as well. Our health is affected by how much physical activity we get, the foods we choose and how we prepare them, whether or not we smoke, how many hours of sleep we allow ourselves, and the ways we deal with stress. In fact, mounting evidence suggests that positive habits can sometime override unfortunate genet-ics. Many people who take excellent care of themselves never develop or significantly delay the arrival of the diabetes or heart disease that plagued their parents and grandparents. Few gifts to our child may be more important that helping her or him develop the habits that set the stage for a lifetime of their best possible health.

The key message here: Exceptional parents consistently prac-tice habits that support their optimal health and teach these habits to their child so he or she can make them their own. Believe me, I know that this can be challenging in our time-starved, stressed-out world. But it is absolutely vital.

You probably have a good idea of the specific habits I'm talking about. Not wanting to get preachy and also recognizing that to do the topic real justice would require an entire book, I share the recommendations that follow as brief reminders. You'll note the special emphasis I give stress.

- Eat and offer your child whole, minimally processed foods. Organic foods, those untouched by chemical fertilizers, pesticides, and preservatives, make the very best choices, but, because organic food generally costs more than that produced by so-called "conventional" methods, this option may be beyond the reach of many families' budgets.

- Drink lots of water—many health experts suggest at least eight 8 ounce glasses each day, or half a gallon. Stay away from drinks laden with sugar and artificial flavors. Children easily learn to prefer water and natural juices and unsweetened tea if they are never offered products with added sugar. Those who have not become accustomed to these products tend to find them sickeningly sweet.

- Remember that the purpose of food is to nourish your body. Some people find it helpful to equate food with *fuel*. When you think of food this way, it may become a bit easier to resist using food for comfort, as a pastime, or entertainment. (Regarding that last word, I attended a lecture years ago at which the speaker, a developmental psychologist, advised parents to teach their children that treats like donuts and ice cream are "entertainment" rather than food. He talked about how well this approach worked with his own kids, who learned to taste sweet treats for fun but rarely ate more than a few bites. Food for thought indeed.)

- If overeating challenges you, as it does so many people, consider attending Weight Watchers. While I generally avoid

Ken Dolan-Del Vecchio

making direct recommendations of this sort, I make an exception here. Weight Watchers has a long record of helping people achieve healthy eating habits. Many friends, family members and clients sing this program's praises. The key to maintaining healthy weight will not likely come from a time-limited diet that restricts certain foods, over-emphasizes others and promises miracles. Instead, a healthy weight results from a sustained habit of eating nutritious food in reasonable amounts. Weight Watchers offers the wisdom and support to help you get there.

- Offer your child the amount of food that helps him or her remain within their optimum weight range. Pay close attention to your pediatrician's recommendations and follow them carefully if your child leans toward being either overweight or underweight.

- Let go of the belief that running, weight lifting and other strenuous forms of exercise provide the *only* path to optimum health. While these fit some character styles, they may not fit yours. Instead of *working out*, it helps many people to simply *move more*. Try taking the stairs rather than the elevator and walking a bit more. I have a friend who carried more than a hundred pounds of extra body weight until just last year, when he saw a physician expressly about his obesity, got serious about getting healthy, and lost over 70 pounds. He now makes a habit of parking far away from the door to his office building, the grocery store and other places he visits regularly. "My kids tell me how relieved they are about my weight loss—they were afraid I could die at any moment from a stroke or heart attack."

- Walk, hike and do other outdoor activities with your child. Help them experience the joy and other good feelings that come with being physically active.

- Never underestimate the importance of getting adequate rest. Study after study confirms the health benefits associated with sleeping at least seven hours every night, yet relatively few adults actually allow themselves this amount of rest. My schedule finds me in the office at 7 a.m. and I hit the gym for 90 minutes every morning before I get there (I am one of those people for whom lifting weights and running have become lifelong habits). In order to keep this schedule, I need to get out of bed by 4:30 a.m. Consequently, I try to be in bed by 8:30 p.m. each evening. (I can't always make this happen but I do my best to follow this routine.) My schedule has long been fodder for jokes made by friends and family. I have one friend who, whenever we're speaking on the phone after 8 p.m., tells me, "Wow, this is like 3 a.m. for you, I feel honored that you're talking to me at this hour."

- Help your child get the amount of rest that keeps them feeling awake and energetic during the daytime. For most children this means at least eight hours. Teens often do well with a bit more. Setting and keeping your child to a schedule for bedtime and waking up ("lights out" and "up and out of your bedroom" times for teens) can set up a healthy pattern that will serve them for a long time to come.

- Stress kills. Please take this seriously. You deserve to live without unhealthy levels of stress, as does every member of your family.

  — Stress overload worsens every health challenge that comes your way. It weakens your immune system, making you more vulnerable to everything from the common cold to clinical depression to heart disease. All of the above suggestions can help limit your stress overload, along with habits such as taking a few minutes every couple of hours to relax and breathe deeply, making a list at the start of each day of the top four or five things you want to accomplish (and checking them off as you achieve them), and making sure you regularly spend time with people who are special to you.

— Help your child adjust their activities according to their own experiences with stress. Some people naturally have a lower stress threshold than others. Help your child choose after-school and weekend activities with an eye toward avoiding overload. Also, help them to recognize and back away from toxic friendships, and respond healthily to pressures related to grades and peer relationships.

— Bear in mind that not all stress creates harm. Think of stress as the way your body and mind respond to any change or challenge. Stress equals the experience of gearing up to do what's necessary; it's an entirely normal feature of everyday life. The goal, therefore, is not to try to eliminate stress, but rather to seek a level of stress that suits your temperament. Some people—emergency room medical team members, for example—may relish a high degree of change and challenge. They may feel most engaged when responding to a crisis. Others, people who earn their living crafting exquisite pottery or proofreading books, may prefer calmer and predictable circumstances. It pays to identify when we're experiencing too much or too little stress, and then do what will help restore the balance that fits our particular nature.

— The same holds true for your child. One child may relish challenges that another child would abhor. You can help your child identify how he or she feels about the opportunities before them, and how best to respond given their particular temperament.

— When we experience too much stress, we may need to reduce the hours or intensity of energy we devote to work or another area of life. At the same time, we may increase our involvement with calming activities such as meditation, prayer, listening to music, taking walks and spending time with loved ones.

— When we feel bored or "numbed out" by the stress of inactivity, it makes sense to seek opportunities that will bring new positive stresses. These may include volunteer work that challenges us to learn new things and meet new people, adult learning classes that engage our intellect and creativity, and team sports that reignite passions we've let slip away. The key to managing stress lies in paying attention to how we feel, finding the courage to set limits on behaviors that no longer serve us well, and engaging in new, healthier ones. We owe it to our child to teach them these things as we practice them ourselves.

As I noted earlier, you've undoubtedly heard much of this advice before. The challenge, as with so much else that we've discussed, lies in the doing. The pressures and temptations around us make it easy to stuff ourselves with unhealthy-but-fast food, spend too many of our waking hours sitting, deprive ourselves of much-needed sleep, and tolerate unhealthy measures of stress. Practicing healthy habits, therefore, often requires courage, determination and discipline. Staying connected to other health-conscious adults can go a long way toward helping you stay on track. Stick with it. The health benefits for both you and your child will be worth the effort.

Key points:
1. Exceptional parents consistently practice habits that support their best possible physical health, teaching these habits to their child as they reinforce them through their own example.
2. Eating well, engaging in regular physical activity (not necessarily traditional forms of exercise), getting enough sleep and managing stress are among the most important health habits.
3. Practicing these habits consistently may require courage, determination and discipline as we are surrounded by pressures and temptations toward less healthy options.

Ken Dolan-Del Vecchio

4. Support from like-minded friends and family members can prove immensely valuable so, as with all goals, tell your friends what you're doing to keep yourself well (you may even want to invite them to join you). Ask them to check in with you on how well you're keeping these habits going and offer to provide the same kind of support with loving accountability for them.

Knowing the Facts about Addiction

No discussion on health and parenting would be complete without mentioning addiction. Addiction wreaks havoc in the lives of adults and teenagers, and results in far too many avoidable deaths. Research findings vary, with some determining that as little as 7 percent and others as much as 60 percent of the general population struggle with at least one addiction. But experience convinces me that few families escape this scourge entirely.

Despite its extraordinary prevalence, addiction remains in the shadows. Human beings have a long history of shaming those who suffer from poorly understood health conditions—think leprosy, cancer and AIDS. Addiction shares this legacy. Long misunderstood as evidence of moral weakness, today experts recognize addiction as a medical condition. Hopefully, we will soon arrive at a time when *no* health problem casts the shadow of stigma over those who suffer.

We rarely shake off history easily, however. While mainstream culture may no longer openly humiliate those recovering from addiction and other behavioral health conditions, many people who experience them personally carry the old shaming messages deep inside. It takes a special kind of courage to acknowledge this health condition and begin the work of healing.

The key message here: Exceptional parents know the warning signs of addiction, pay attention to their own behavior and, perhaps even more importantly, listen respectfully to any expressions of concern from loved ones. The last point is extraordinarily important because the afflicted person rarely identifies his or her own addiction. Instead, the challenge of identification and bringing the difficult news to the addict typically falls to loved ones.

Exceptional parents also speak freely with their children about addiction, describing what it is, mentioning family members who struggle with this illness without expressing negative judgment about them and inviting their child to ask questions. They also ask questions if their child's behavior suggests that he or she may have a problem and, as needed, will seek professional assistance for their child.

It is important to acknowledge here that many people use substances without becoming addicted. Many adults drink alcohol and take prescribed mind-altering drugs without harmful results. Others misuse or abuse such substances. They occasionally drink to excess or use prescription or illegal substances "recreationally." The big distinction between these behaviors and addiction: Addiction causes harmful consequences to self and/or others. The best information available shows that most people who become addicted came into the world with a brain-based sensitivity to mind-altering substances that is not found in those who do not become addicted.

Addictions may involve behaviors that include (but aren't limited to) substance use, gambling, overspending, excessive time on the Internet, use of pornography and sexual activity. Over time, the behavior increasingly consumes time and energy, overriding sound judgment in ways that damage one or more important aspects of life. Addictive behavior often damages work or school performance as well as family relationships, including the ability to parent. It can damage health, financial security and safety. Addiction also frequently results in legal problems such as arrests for driving while intoxicated or for illicit drug use.

The addictive behavior takes on a life of its own, progressively growing worse and making the addict's life increasingly unmanageable. By "takes on a life of its own" I mean that the addict experiences the addictive behavior as something that operates beyond their control. The person with an addiction feels as though the addiction possesses them, compelling them to buy the particular substance or carry out the behavior to which they are addicted, despite their best intentions to quit. He or she may want desperately to stop gambling but still drive to Atlantic City and start loading quarters into a slot machine. A person addicted to the Internet may desperately want to shut down their computer or phone and get some sleep but will keep surfing the net all night long. The clinical term for this behavior is compulsion. The person with an addiction is driven by a compulsion—an urge that feels impossible to disobey—to use the substance or perform the behavior in question.

Two additional hallmarks of the illness are denial and irrationality. Addicts will swear they can control their addictive behavior despite all evidence to the contrary. An alcoholic will insist that every one of the seven drinks she swallows in one evening will be her very last, and she will sincerely mean what she says each and every time. The irrationality here will elude her. This pattern marks the behavior of all addicts, whether their compulsion involves substances, gambling, overeating, sexual acting out, some other destructive behavior or a combination of several such behaviors (as is often the case).

The addict's irrationality and denial sometimes gets reflected in, and unwittingly encouraged by, the behavior of others. The word *enabling* captures this phenomenon. An employee smells of alcohol and nods off nearly every afternoon, staggers and slurs his words, and regularly calls out sick on Mondays and Fridays. Colleagues and supervisors give him space, make excuses for his strange behavior, and refrain from confronting his diminished job performance. None of this helps, of course. Enabling allows the addict to continue spiraling downward, increasingly endangering themselves and others.

It's no fun to confront an employee who reports to you at work on their performance problems and it's no fun to confront a loved one with the damage their behavior does; but the alternative, saying nothing while they continue to destroy themselves and possibly hurt many others along the way, serves nobody's interest.

When parents make a commitment to stay aware of their own potentially addictive patterns and accept help as needed, we provide a healthy example for our child. Whether or not we ourselves are in recovery from addiction, we owe it to our child to pay attention to their behavior and respond actively to any of these warning signs:

- Behavior that suggests intoxication: slurred speech, stumbling, sluggishness, alcohol smell on the breath, bloodshot eyes, smell of marijuana, strange displays of emotion (laughing uncontrollably, flashes of anger, nodding off, blank staring).
- A pattern of secrecy and lying.
- Increased moodiness and irritability.
- Withdrawal from previous level of social involvement with family, friends who you consider a good influence and positive community activities (their community of faith, for example).
- A negative shift in attitude toward, and performance in, school or work.
- Increased absences from school or work.
- Apathy, low energy and lack of enthusiasm for activities that used to be of great interest.
- Less attention to personal grooming.
- Stealing from family members.
- New friends that strike you as poor role models.

Each of these warrants at least a heartfelt conversation to learn more about what's going on. And if any of these occur with sustained and increasing intensity it makes sense to have your child speak with their physician or a psychotherapist who is knowledgeable regarding addiction. There will be no harm done by "over-responding" if it turns out that no addiction problem exists, although you may have

Ken Dolan-Del Vecchio

to help your child understand your concern and talk through their feelings about it—quite possibly including some degree of anger. Nonetheless, as has often been said, it's better to be safe than sorry.

Just yesterday my team at work concluded our Health and Wellness organization's annual meeting. During a break, I noticed a colleague poring through a document on his electronic reading device. I asked what he was reading. He shared that he was reviewing the life insurance death claim for a 24-year-old who had overdosed on heroin. As both of us have twenty-something children, we talked briefly about how common heroin abuse and deaths by overdose have become in recent years.

Prescription painkiller abuse is rife at the moment. Addiction cases such as the one my colleague shared too frequently begin when an adolescent or young adult child tries prescription painkillers found in their parent's medicine cabinet. In most cases, parents use their own medications responsibly. Still, we owe it to ourselves and our children to address our own addictive behavior if and when it occurs. We need to be role models of health and recovery.

Key points:
1. Exceptional parents know the warning signs of addiction, pay attention to their own behavior and, perhaps more importantly, listen respectfully to expressions of concern from loved ones.
2. Addiction is an illness and no more indicative of moral failure or bad character than diabetes, heart disease or any other medical condition.
3. Compulsion, denial and irrationality, hallmarks of addiction, make it unlikely that the afflicted person will identify their illness unless confronted by others.
4. Usually, it falls to people close to the addict to confront him or her with the reality of their addiction. Therefore, it's important for parents to know the warning signs and talk forthrightly with their child if the child's behavior raises concern.

5. When parents, other loved ones, coworkers and others close to the person with an addiction shoulder the addict's responsibilities and in other ways participate in denying their illness, this enables the addict and helps nobody. Sometimes parents, for example, write untruthful excuses for their child's absence at school, give them money that they know will most likely be used to buy alcohol or drugs, and explain away their absences at important family events.

6. Effective help is available from professional treatment providers, and 12-step communities offer tremendous and often life-changing social support. Your primary care physician can refer you to a treatment provider or you can look online for the contact information of one the many addiction treatment programs available. Information on12-step program meetings can also be found online.

7. People with addictions, exceptional parents and their children alike, owe it to themselves (and their loved ones) to get the help that will support their entry into recovery.

Taking Care of Your Mental Health

Having spent time discussing addiction, it makes sense to also address depression and other mental health conditions. While I don't want to belabor the subject of behavioral health, I also don't want to avoid it. Suicide, the most dangerous consequence of depression, kills far too many people, including children, every year.

This tragic fact stings even more when we consider the effectiveness of modern treatments for mental illness, which usually involve a combination of talk therapy, medication, and, increasingly, physical exercise and nutrition. When it comes to depression, 80 percent of those who seek treatment will benefit enormously. Unfortunately, at least a third of those who meet the criteria for the illness never seek the help they need and deserve.

We're talking about vast numbers of people. Depression strikes nearly one in every 10 people worldwide. According to a World Health Organization report published in 2015, it is the leading cause of disability worldwide. Severity varies. At the lesser end of the spectrum, depression casts a cloud of negativity over nearly every experience, thought, and emotion, robbing the individual of vibrancy and joy. At its worst, depression can cause such anguish that the sufferer takes self-destructive action.

Key symptoms of depression center on a negative mood that persists for two weeks or more. This mood can take the form of despair, lack of energy, apathy and/or irritability. Often the person who suffers feels nothing positive—not even a hint of joy—for that length of time and even longer. In addition, depression can bring difficulty concentrating, short-term memory problems, sleeping too much or too little, and eating too much or too little.

Other types of mental illness occur with great frequency as well. They include post-traumatic stress disorder (PTSD), other anxiety problems, illnesses that distort thinking and behavior, such as obsessive-compulsive disorder, and mood disorders other than depression, including bipolar disorder.

While some mental illnesses typically show themselves for the first time during late adolescence, including bipolar affective disorder and schizophrenia, developmental disorders such as Asperger Syndrome and other conditions on the autism spectrum, problems with negative mood, excessive fear (anxiety), and compulsive behavior may show up much earlier. Our child deserves help from a carefully chosen professional for any persistently upsetting mood or pattern of thinking.

The key message here: Exceptional parents take care of all aspects of their health, including their mental health. They also recognize when their child feels emotional distress that goes beyond the usual ups and downs and seek help from the child's pediatrician or a psychotherapist.

Let me introduce you to one of my heroes. Dr. Shirley Cresci works as director of Behavioral Health Services on my team at Prudential. She leads a group of eight behavioral health professionals who provide employees with mental health assessment, brief counseling, referrals, life coaching, leadership consulting and customized training. Shirley also represents our Health and Wellness organization on Prudential's Incident Oversight Team, which addresses situations that show warning signs for workplace violence. The Incident Oversight Team includes professionals from Human Resources, Global Security and Prudential's Law Department. Shirley has a big job and she has been doing it exceptionally well for close to a decade now. She also has a history of living with depression and anxiety.

Last year, Shirley appeared in a short film produced at Prudential. In it, she describes her experiences with depression and anxiety, the way she learned about available help, and how participating in treatment has restored her joy in life and kept her healthy. In the video, Shirley also notes the irony of living through the challenges presented by mental illness while also serving as director of a behavioral health services program that provides care to more than 20,000 employees and their family members. The video's goal was to break the stigma that lingers around mental illness and encourage employees to seek help when they experience symptoms.

Shirley's forthrightness and courage have gone a long way toward achieving this goal. The film has been viewed by thousands of Prudential employees, a number of whom have called or written emails to Shirley thanking her for her courage and letting her know that she inspired them to seek help for the very first time. One of Shirley's two adult sons works at Prudential as well. Shirley told me how meaningful it was to hear him say, after viewing the video, "I'm proud of you, mom."

As I've mentioned many times, everything we do teaches our children something about how to live. When we address health challenges, including signs of mental illness, and help our child do the same, we provide invaluable assistance and an important life lesson.

Key points:

1. Exceptional parents take care of all aspects of their health, including their mental health. They seek help when not feeling well and follow through with the recommendations provided by professional helpers.
2. Exceptional parents pay attention to their child's emotional health and seek assistance if needed, just as they would for any other health concern.
3. Depression is not just feeling "a bit down." It's a serious medical condition that, if left untreated, can be lethal.
4. Treatment for depression and many other mental illnesses is highly effective.
5. Far from being a sign of weakness, asking for help demonstrates strength and wisdom. We can assist our child in developing this capacity by our own example as well as by readily getting help for our child, if needed. Asking for assistance is one of life's most important skills.

Making Sex an Open Secret

Like many parents in the 1950s and early 1960s, mine kept mum on this subject. Not only did they say nothing, they also managed to keep hidden from my two older brothers and me almost every affectionate touch they exchanged. In retrospect, it's hard to imagine how the three of us got here, considering how platonic their relationship appeared.

I learned about human reproduction in those peculiar junior high school classes familiar to most people of my generation. Here, the merger of sperm and egg, followed by the stages of embryonic development, were described in some detail. However, the story of how sperm and egg found themselves in the same locale was left to our youthful imaginations.

I learned about sex in the way that boys traditionally do, through pornography. In my case, this meant *Penthouse* and *Playboy* magazines pilfered mostly from the "hidden" stashes of my two best friends' father and brother, respectively. Volumes have been written about how pornography teaches us to see human beings as objects and sex as a means for personal gratification, with little or no consideration for the needs and feelings of the other participant. Volumes have also been written about the challenges involved in trying to unlearn this way of thinking when we actually start having sex with real-life human beings. When we don't learn positive attitudes toward sexuality and intimacy in childhood and adolescence, people of all genders are at risk for much unnecessary pain.

Exceptional parents save their child a world of trouble through honest conversations about sexuality and modeling respectful and loving interaction with their own partner, should they have one. They demonstrate perspectives that break not only the code of silence on the subject, but also mainstream culture's rigid attitudes about gender, physical attractiveness and related topics. Physical, emotional, and spiritual security, along with joy and respect for oneself and others—the essentials of self-love—become their guiding themes.

Let me introduce you to a couple who role model these qualities. Janet and Bill, a couple in their mid-50s, live in New Jersey. They have two young adult children, Barbara and Paul. Barbara, age 30, lives in Oregon with her husband, Josh, and their 2-year old son. Paul, 21, is finishing his final year in college. Eight years ago, concern regarding Paul brought Janet and Bill to me for therapy. We resolved this concern and I've consulted with the family periodically since then.

Janet and Bill demonstrate much strength when it comes to supporting their children's healthy sexuality. They strike an ideal balance, making the subject visible, open for conversation as needed, and bounded by limits that respect everyone's privacy.

Ken Dolan-Del Vecchio

One of the first things I noticed after meeting Bill and Janet was their easy closeness with one another. They pulled their chairs together in the consulting room and frequently touched in ways that conveyed love and support—a hand reaching out to touch the other's knee or shoulder, patting and holding one another's hands, and sharing a hug and kiss at the end of particularly challenging conversations.

Bill, who was overweight, talked about his efforts to lose 20 pounds. Both he and Janet noted that this was a health concern. In sessions that included only the two of them, they also mentioned that, as much as they loved one another and enjoyed an active sex life, the extra pounds made Bill doubt his own attractiveness. Janet, a fitness buff who was in extraordinary physical condition, gingerly agreed that losing weight would make Bill even more appealing to her. I have seen few people talk about such a charged subject with as much candor and mutual support as they did.

The couple's ease and honesty with one another was reflected in their son's relationship to his own sexuality. Paul had always been allowed to talk on the phone and electronically only to people who were schoolmates or members of the family's faith community. People whom he had never met in person were off-limits. Paul's parents noticed that he'd always made friends more easily with girls and spent almost all of his free time talking and visiting with girls. This trend continued, yet by age 13 Paul hadn't mentioned any interest in dating or attending dances. Bill and Janet told Paul their observations and asked him if he was attracted to girls or boys or both. Bill and Janet told me that this conversation with Paul took place in an entirely matter-of-fact way, as though they were discussing any other feelings that their son may have.

During one session with all three of them, Paul said. "Mom and dad wondered if I'm gay or straight or bi and I told them that I'm straight. I also told them that I'm not so interested in hanging out with other guys because, aside from playing football with them,

152

which is fun, I feel like I can't have much of a real conversation with guys my age. So hanging out with them doesn't do much for me."

As Paul began high school he started dating and attending dances. He, Bill and Janet reported that they engaged in a series of family conversations about the importance of treating girls with respect. The family also talked about the importance of connecting sexual behavior with love and respect. Paul's older sister, Barbara, told Paul that most, though not all, women see sex as part of a meaningful relationship and aren't that into "hooking up" just for sex.

During an individual meeting with Janet, she told me about Barbara's early years. "Barbara and Paul are different when it comes to lots of things, including the way they approach sex," she said. "Paul's style has always been more reserved." Janet said that Barbara, on the other hand, had asked her parents questions about where babies came from when she was 3 and what masturbation is when she was 6. "We gave her the most complete answers we thought would make sense for a kid her age and always emphasized the positive." Janet said, "I remember telling Barbara that masturbation feels good but it's a private thing, and it's polite to do it only when you're in your room by yourself. I added that later on, when she was all grown up and in a loving relationship with someone very special to her, they might do it together in their bedroom. I felt pretty weird saying this kind of stuff, but I was determined to give my kids real information instead of letting them wander into their own fantasies without any help at all."

Janet shared with me that she told her own mother about these conversations with Barbara. "My mother said she was proud of me for having this kind of frank discussion with my daughter. I'll always remember that."

Paul's parents provided him with condoms and told him to ask for more if he needed them. They talked with one another and with trusted friends about questions that arose. One that they brought to my attention involved a girl Paul was dating casually while a senior in high school. Paul had told his father that she wanted them to have sex but he was holding back so far because he didn't have really strong feelings for her. "On the other hand," he told Bill, "she's incredibly hot." Bill assured Paul that he understood his mixed feelings, sharing a story from his own teenage years. He also told his son how great it felt to have Paul trust him with this dilemma. They talked about how powerful sex is and how, while Paul would probably feel better ultimately if he abstained this time, Bill had some idea how hard it may be to decline the offer. They talked about how this invitation presented an important learning experience for both Paul and the young woman involved.

Bill and Janet addressed their children's emerging sexuality by giving calm, understanding, age-appropriate information, asking clarifying but not intrusive questions, and offering solid support. Throughout his growing years, they conveyed an attitude of trust along with the expectation that Paul, like all of us, will take missteps here and there that will provide valuable learning experiences. One of the most impressive aspects of this couple's caring for their children was their willingness to seek counsel from professionals and, perhaps even more importantly, from friends and family members whom they love and respect. And they did so in ways always respectful of their children. Janet and Bill understand the extraordinary value gained by tapping into this reservoir of wisdom and good will.

During one of our final meetings I asked Janet and Bill where they learned about the usefulness of asking for help. Each of them described how lucky they were to have parents who were willing to talk about challenging subjects with their kids and willing to ask for help with their own life challenges. Almost simultaneously they told me that their motto is "*When in doubt, talk it out.*" Janet added, "Look, life is complicated. Kids are complicated. Sex is complicated. It would be foolish to go it alone when other people have so many good ideas to offer."

Key points:
1. Exceptional parents give their child accurate information about sex in words that fit their child's age and ability to understand. They also model respectful and loving interaction with their own partner if they have one.
2. Sex is a fundamentally important part of life. Exceptional parents make the subject visible, open for conversation as needed, and bounded by limits that respect everyone's privacy.
3. With this and all other important subjects, it can help to gain information and recommendations from people whom you love and respect, as well as professional sources.
4. When parents don't provide guidance, their child defaults to the available sources of information: their peers, internet pornography, and images and stories from other popular media. (No child deserves to be without parental guidance amid *this* mix of information sources!)

Showing Them the Money

Call to mind someone you know who has money trouble. I think of a friend, a highly-credentialed educator who taught for decades at a private high school. A year ago, his employer eliminated his job without any advance notice. Having saved nothing over his many years of employment, he now finds himself spared homelessness only by the generosity of members of his community of faith.

Another friend earns well over $150,000 annually as a managing partner in a small business and from her side work as a consultant. She spends freely on high-status automobiles, dinners out, home furnishings and other consumer goods. Now in her late 50s, she has no appreciable savings, a minimal pension and no idea how she would survive were she to stop working. She recently told me that her 26-year-old daughter earns $15 per hour as a retail salesperson, has maxed out two credit cards, and was recently told by her boyfriend that she spends so much that he doesn't feel safe taking the next step toward engagement. My friends and their family members are far from alone here. In *The Secret Shame of Middle-Class Americans*, an article by Neil Garber published in the April 18, 2016, edition of *The Atlantic*, the author reports that nearly half of Americans would have trouble finding $400 to pay for an emergency.

What if every parent understood that showing their child how to manage money may likely spare them such pain? (I say "likely," because circumstances far beyond our control can arise, particularly in a society in which healthcare crises can become financial crises as well.) What if we recognized that we may offer the only voice of sound judgment standing between our child and a world gone berserk with consumerism, a world that barrages our child endlessly with media messages beseeching them to make unnecessary purchases?

Exceptional parents get it. They buck the consumerist norm by effectively managing their money and teaching their child the habits that make this possible. Specifically, they understand the difference between needs and wants and make choices accordingly. They handle credit carefully and when they earn more than their family's needs require they save and invest with an eye toward long-term security. Finally, they value real financial security more than they value projecting the illusion of wealth through display of expensive cars, clothing and other products.

My work as a therapist convinces me that doing these things takes courage and a rare capacity to break with the herd. It all begins with an honest look at our own financial situation. This may sound simple but, like so many other habits, simple in concept doesn't mean *easy to do*. In fact, many adults avoid having an honest conversation with *themselves* about money, say nothing about broaching this subject with another person. Openly discussing money, it seems to me, is the final taboo, for most people will speak more freely about the details of their sexual behavior than their financial behavior. Even helping professionals—therapists, counselors, psychiatrists, and social workers—echo this pattern, comfortably asking questions about every conceivable personal habit, except those having to do with money.

The money taboo has everything to do with power. Nothing more precisely reveals where we stand within our culture's *power over* hierarchy than the amount of money we have. When talking about money, therefore, we risk extraordinary vulnerability. But if we don't teach our children about money through our example and through direct information sharing—if we don't allow ourselves to be vulnerable with our child in this way—we leave them with no sound guidance amid a swarm of messages designed to lead them astray.

Erik knows all there is to know about my finances and his mom's. We have talked regularly about saving, investing and living below our means, a lifelong practice for Lynn and me and something we learned from our own parents.

My parents were savers. As middle school teachers, they never earned large salaries and received neither financial help from their parents nor an inheritance. A decade before her death, however, my mother had $300,000, enough, along with her pension and Social Security payments, to sustain her through her later years.

Following my parents' example, I learned to save and invest in mutual funds once I had an emergency fund plus a small amount of money that I didn't need to spend on necessities. Mom and dad were frugal, purchasing cars only when their current vehicle was no longer reparable, eating at restaurants rarely, and vacationing locally for the most part. They researched major purchases carefully. *Consumer Reports* was staple reading in our household.

My parents also encouraged their children to work. My brothers and I each held part-time jobs, starting with newspaper routes in our early teens. The three of us worked hard and got promotions, eventually driving the vans that delivered newspaper bundles to delivery boys and girls and working within the newspaper distributor's office. We learned the connection between work and money, and the importance of managing our meager earnings with care.

Lynn, Erik's mom, comes from a class background similar to mine. Lynn's mother worked as a nurse. Her father started out as a New York City sanitation worker and ultimately advanced to the position of Chief of Collection and Snow Removal for the entire city.

Lynn has an extraordinary aptitude for money management. Her initiative led us to purchase our first home when we were 25. I learned a great deal from her discipline and foresight regarding personal money management. While we are no longer together as a couple, we have both shared our relationship with money and our strategies for managing it with Erik.

Erik knows that I recently reached a major financial goal in my investments portfolio, and he knows the amount of income that my financial planner has told my husband and me that we must earn per year for the next 10 years in order to completely retire from paid employment. Erik knows that I achieved this level of financial security by steadily contributing as much as possible to my 401(k) and SEP IRA across all of my years of working, and saving some beyond those tax-deferred accounts as well. He knows that I have greater skill at saving than choosing investments and, consequently, that I rely on financial services professionals to guide my investment allocations.

It has not always been easy resisting the maelstrom of seductive advertising and the pressure to keep up with neighbors, friends and colleagues when it comes to cars, houses and clothes. A friend recently told me, tongue-in-cheek, "You can't drive that car of yours (a 2003 Honda Accord that's logged 286,000 miles and is showing its age) to a business event because anybody who sees it will think you're crazy, which I know is just fine with you. It would be okay, though, if you got a new Prius—and I recommend the dark blue color. That would work because then they'll think you're being green instead of just being cheap. But your old Honda has got to go." This friend's counsel aside, my much-loved Honda is still going strong.

All indications suggest that Erik will carry on the careful money management habits of his parents. He recently told me that he's putting 10 percent of his paycheck into his 401(k) account and will increase his contribution to 15 percent, the amount many financial planners recommend, if he gets a pay raise.

For the past eight years, our Health and Wellness team at Prudential has been helping employees break the money taboo, talk about their relationship with money and build their personal money management skills. Personal budget coaching, a program we launched at Prudential in the spring of 2009 as the "Great Recession" unfolded across the world, helps participants take an honest look at their income, spending and saving habits and, from there, work toward achieving their best possible financial health.

Mike DiMaio, a longtime friend and colleague whose background includes finance, ministry, and coaching, delivers this program. You couldn't find someone better suited to the task. In my mind's eye, I see Mike's smiling face as I write these words. Everything this man says, and the warm and cheerful way in which he says it shows that he wants the best for each of us, that he cares. And because he wants what's best for his clients, Mike doesn't hesitate to tell the truth about what he sees. In the most loving way, he tells his personal budget coaching clients when they're deceiving themselves by denying reality and avoiding the hard decisions suggested by their financial circumstances. He gives them the tools and support that help them course-correct.

"I've learned over the years of giving seminars on personal money management and doing this coaching that many people, no matter how large their incomes, are only one or two paychecks away from financial catastrophe." I've heard Mike say this many times. I've also heard him lament the fact that personal money management almost never gets taught in our schools. "This isn't rocket science, but the emotions and confusion surrounding money make it into a monumental challenge for a lot of people," Mike has said.

Having dinner with a friend recently, we caught each other up on our young-adult children, both of whom had recently graduated from college and were working part-time while seeking full-time jobs. I shared with her a story that Erik had told me recently. My son mentioned that one of his best friend's parents had given their son $30,000 to buy a new car after his old one fell terminally ill. Erik said he convinced his friend to buy a used car costing less than half of the monetary gift, and then invest the other half in mutual funds. My dining partner told me that her daughter was similarly frugal, living at home, paying off student debt and at the same time saving part of every paycheck.

While my dinner companion and I have positive stories to share about our children's relationship with money, and many other young people are similarly financially responsible (a significant portion of the so-called millennial generation handle their money with care), Mike assures me that this is not always the case. As a parent, your role modeling, as well as your willingness to speak openly about personal money management, can help your child prepare to build their own financial security.

Key points:
1. Exceptional parents manage their money and teach their child the habits that will help them do the same.
2. It's important for us teach our kids personal money management because our schools rarely teach these skills.
3. Talking openly about money breaks an important taboo. It opens the way for your child to learn about personal money management and empowers them to seek help as needed with this important aspect of life throughout their adult years.

Chapter 5
Reflections and Rewards

Your life is now.
—John Mellencamp, singer-songwriter

We have memories and we have plans, but the only time we truly have is *now*, this very moment. I'm spending mine typing these words. You're reading them. There will never be a better time to write, read, reflect and show love to our children. What came before is history. History leaves us gifts and consequences. We can learn from it. It can help us shape what we do now, but I am not bound to my history and you are not bound to yours.

Never Too Late

"I was a terrible parent," my friend, Dana, recently confided. We were finishing dinner and had just ordered coffee. She continued in a soft tone, "I was too young and my ex-husband and I had no idea what we were doing. We did the best we could but we argued a lot, made each other unhappy, and had weird relationships with our son. His father treated him like his best buddy rather than his child, and I was too strict and overprotective most of the time. Steven became a sweet, loving young man, but he never really grew up. At 32 he still doesn't handle adult responsibilities well. He can't seem to keep a job and goes from one relationship to the next. He gets bored, the person he's dating becomes old news and he moves on. If I had it to do over again, I'd do lots of things differently." Dana shifted in her chair and fixed her eyes on her coffee cup.

Most parents have regrets about things we did or didn't do, especially those of us who take parenting seriously. This makes sense, for those who strive to do things right almost always harp on what they *should, could, or would have* done even better. Conscientious people tend to judge themselves harshly.

As I listened to my friend, I couldn't help but notice how she glided past her description of her son as a "sweet, loving young man." While he may find it difficult to stay in a job and he may never seem to find an enduring intimate relationship—both of which may involve complexities beyond any one person's control—Steven's sweet and loving nature deserved more emphasis, in my opinion. I asked Dana to say more about it.

Dana talked about Steven's devotion to his elderly grandparents, how he regularly stops by to visit them at the assisted living center where they live, often bearing gifts of their favorite foods. She went on to describe how respectfully he approaches both her and his father. She also mentioned the loving care Steven gives his two cats.

I asked her how this young man learned such behavior, having grown up in a world that's still full of messages that teach boys and men to view gentleness as weakness. Could Dana and his father have had something to do with it? I asked that Dana consider giving herself credit for raising such a gentleman, while also acknowledging that neither he nor any of us will ever achieve perfection.

As you and I move toward the conclusion of our time together, I ask you, as I asked my friend, Dana, to put your regrets in perspective rather than dwelling on them. I ask you to make a list of the positive things you've done. Use today to do your best for both you and your loved ones. The key message here: We owe it to ourselves and our child, no matter how old or young he or she may be, to put the negative in perspective, take stock of what's good in our lives, and then work to create even more of it.

This seems a good moment also to put exceptional parenting itself in proper perspective. A parent may do everything I've described in this book and still their child may behave in ways that don't serve them at all well. On the other hand, we may have practiced none of the habits described here and our now-adult child enjoys a deeply fulfilling life. The alchemy of human behavior remains complex and mysterious. Exceptional parenting undoubtedly benefits children but many other influences, including genetic inheritance, our child's peer network, other community factors, and a host of individual personality attributes also contribute to their development. In truth, we can take neither full credit nor full blame for the adult our child becomes.

That said, there remains every reason to continue striving to create a fulfilling life for ourselves and also become the best possible parent to our child. I have counseled many clients who wish things were different in their own lives or in their relationships with their adult and near-adult children. The keys to success here include respect for personal boundaries, empathy, consistently loving action and patience, alongside the awareness that the past is unchangeable and the present moment is the only one in which new possibilities can come alive.

At 47, Chaim was working to re-establish his life and livelihood in the aftermath of his divorce from Arlene. The couple had a 19-year-old son, Mordecai, a sophomore in college who lived on campus not far from Chaim's apartment. Chaim reported that there had never been physical violence or name-calling between Arlene and him, but they had disagreed irreconcilably about almost everything for as long as he could remember. They went through cycles in which bickering gave way to long periods of painful silence. When Mordecai entered college, Chaim and Arlene decided they'd had enough. They decided to divorce.

The couple owned and operated a small stationery store that had been in Chaim's family since its founding by his grandfather in 1935. When they separated, Chaim bought Arlene out of the business and began working even longer hours managing the store. Hoping to augment his income, Chaim had also recently begun training to become a financial services professional. He planned to hire a store manager if he could make a go of this new profession.

Chaim consulted with me after recognizing, as the post-divorce dust settled, that he and his son had almost no relationship. During all those years of arguing with Arlene and working at the shop, Mordecai had grown to adulthood with very little contact and interest from his father. During the weeks prior to our consultation, Chaim had three times asked his son to meet for dinner and each time received the response from Mordecai that his courses were so intense that he couldn't spare the time.

Chaim told me that he believed his only choice was to accept that he had lost his son and move on, "leaving the ball in his court."

I advised that his desire to develop a connection with his son was a healthy one and that a serious effort would require giving up his all-or-nothing stance in favor of a more realistic posture of patience, consistency, accountability and respect. I told him that leaving the ball in Mordecai's court was what he'd done all of Mordecai's young life, and learning to live without his dad had been the only solution left to his son. It made sense that Mordecai had little interest in seeing his father, for he had long ago learned to live without him and now had his college coursework calling his attention.

I advised Chaim that the divorce had also likely stirred emotions within Mordecai (who had not shared any of his reactions to the breakup with his father), which may also contribute to his current reluctance to see his father.

Chaim began the work of inviting his son into a relationship. He sent Mordecai a text saying he loved him and would love to get together when Mordecai could find time, perhaps over dinner, lunch, breakfast or just coffee. Chaim then wrote a letter of apology to Mordecai in which he took responsibility for his absence from his son's life. He also acknowledged his part in the constant arguing with Mordecai's mother. In his letter, Chaim described the sadness, confusion, loneliness and despair he imagined Mordecai experiencing as he grew up in such a home. Chaim and I reviewed the draft of this letter so I could help to make certain that it did not contain excuses or blame Arlene, but rather focused only on the pain that Chaim imagined his actions had caused Mordecai and his mother. He mailed the letter.

Two weeks later, Chaim received an email from his son. Mordecai thanked Chaim for the letter and agreed to have dinner. Over their meal, Mordecai validated many of the feelings that his father had mentioned within the letter. He asked Chaim how he had managed to disregard his child so completely, saying he always thanked God for his mother, who he'd learned to see as his only parent. Chaim told Mordecai that he could not offer any acceptable answer, as nothing could justify such neglect. As we had discussed,

Chaim's sole purpose in this meeting was to listen and validate his son's experience.

Thereafter, Chaim continued to invite his son to meet with him, always according to his son's availability. Chaim also made certain to acknowledge Mordecai's forthcoming birthday with a card and request time together on that day and the approaching holidays, regardless of whether Mordecai expressed interest in his company.

I cautioned Chaim that any pressuring of Mordecai would likely cause his son to retreat. I suggested that the current approach, with Chaim always molding his availability to Mordecai's schedule, made more sense for months and maybe even years to come. I reminded Chaim that he had made himself unavailable to his son for the 19 years of Mordecai's life when his son most needed his father. Given this history, Mordecai offering any of his time to Chaim showed generosity of spirit, forgiveness and a leap of faith.

I also coached Chaim to build a fuller life for himself. Knowing that he was training to be a financial planner, I asked whether he himself had a financial plan. You can perhaps imagine the answer. He began to develop one. The plan revealed that within a few years, he will need to work fewer hours than he originally imagined necessary.

When Chaim was a young man he'd taken piano lessons and loved the experience. He began taking lessons again and rediscovered his joy in playing. He also began dating and spending more time with old friends. These efforts lessened his despair regarding the past and the pressure he felt to connect with Mordecai. Letting go of this pressure and creating a more vibrant life enlivened the dinner meetings Chaim and Mordecai enjoyed with growing regularity.

Kendra, 58 years old and married, scheduled a time to meet because she felt that she was losing her only child, Bill. At 35, Bill, whose now-deceased father was Kendra's first husband, lived in

Long Island, quite a drive from Kendra's home in New Jersey. Bill and his wife had recently welcomed their first child, Andrea.

Kendra, who worked as an insurance underwriter, complained that Bill and Chris, his partner, had no time for her and didn't seem to care about her desire to see her grandchild.

"They just drove all the way to Portland, Maine, to visit Chris' parents and they can't drive to New Jersey?!" she exclaimed.

As we talked, I learned that Kendra had tried to bring Bill closer to her by complaining that he neglected her. When Kendra continued in this vein after the arrival of her grandchild, Bill told Kendra that she'd be welcome to visit with Andrea but she would have to come visit them and do so on days that fit their schedule. He also told his mother to "get a life," which she found deeply offensive.

After listening to Kendra rail about her ungrateful son, I asked her to tell me more about her larger family. It turned out that both of Kendra's parents had expected her to mold her life around their needs, particularly during their later years. After her husband died, Kendra had spent almost every weekend for several years traveling to Delaware, where her parents lived, to check on them and run their errands. Only after they died did she feel free to pursue a bigger life for herself, eventually marrying her current husband. We talked about the guilt and aggravation she experienced while attending to her parents, and how their demand that she care for them robbed her of the experience of sharing more gentle feelings for them during their final years.

"It's not like they didn't have anyone around them," she said, her voice edged with bitterness. "They went into a progressive care facility and they kept in touch with many of their friends until the very end. They just wanted their daughter doing lots of things for them, presumably because they felt I owed it to them."

I asked Kendra if she saw parallels between what her parents expected from her and what she expected of Bill. She immediately got the connection. I gently told her that Bill was breaking a family pattern by creating a boundary, insisting that his mother respect his needs and those of his growing family. I told her that these requests were healthy, courageous and wise, as was his suggestion that Kendra develop a life of her own. Hearing this, Kendra smiled, something I'd rarely seen her do. She told me it was good to be able to see the positive in what her son was doing instead of taking it personally, as a rejection.

Thereafter, Kendra offered to babysit for Andrea whenever her own schedule and Bill and Chris' needs coincided. She began doing so with some regularity, much to her son's surprise and delight. The more Kendra empathized and responded to the needs of her son and his family, the closer their bond grew. She even thanked Bill for standing up to her. She also told him she was looking around to figure out how she'd spend her time having fun when she was able to retire and "get a life."

Key points:
1. It is never too late to become the best parent that you can be.
2. Remember that the past cannot be changed and the present moment is the only one we ever have.
3. You owe it to yourself and your child, no matter how old or young he or she may be, to put the negative in perspective, take stock of what's good in your life and then work to create even more of it.
4. When interacting with your adult (or near-adult) child, respect their personal boundaries, show empathy and demonstrate consistently loving behavior.

Twenty Years From Now

> Today I shall behave as if this is the day I will be remembered.
>
> —Dr. Seuss

I write these words as our cruise ship prepares to leave Cartagena, Spain, for Barcelona. My husband, our two best friends, and I are four days into our voyage and I'm easing into a state of flow that is familiar from previous vacations. Letting go of the busyness of work, I feel released into a welcome stillness. I'm feeling grateful, for I have in abundance what matters most: good health, loving family and friends. I also feel grateful for the privilege of sharing with you what I've written in this book, my stories and those of my family members, friends, colleagues and clients. I hope they've proved helpful to you.

My meditative mood fits the task of writing this final piece about the gifts of the present moment, the path you and I have traveled together, and the even better future to come. As we move into our last conversation, I'd like to share one more personal reflection. I'm hoping that doing so will invite you to pause, reflect on your own life and maybe even share my reflective mood.

Having reached my 56th birthday, I have seen some of life's typical ups and downs. These include a first marriage that ended amicably after 14 years (my ex-wife is now a dear friend), a second marriage now 19 years strong, the death of my father and, nearly 20 years later, my mother. I've enjoyed a rewarding career that blends family therapy with leadership consulting that promotes organizational health and wellness. As much as I treasure each of these things life has given me, the gift of my son, Erik, stands above the rest. Nothing rivals the gratitude I feel for the privilege of being his father.

I believe that those of us who strive to be exceptional parents place being a mom or dad at the very center of our lives. We undoubtedly fall short in many ways—I know that I do—but we try our best. First and foremost, we try to consistently use our power as *power with*, the power of love rather than domination. We live every day knowing that we'll always rank high among our child's most important role models and strive to promote a positive relationship with them, even during times when he or she may not reciprocate.

Our efforts affirm that parents and children belong to one another like no other human beings do. And whether the connection

Ken Dolan-Del Vecchio

starts biologically or through adoption, *it endures*. It endures even through those times when it may seem to have dissolved. For when children try to leave their parent behind, they usually do so by reacting against the ways their mother or father did things, or, in some cases, by actually severing contact with their parents. Both of these reactions, perhaps paradoxically, charge the relationship with even more emotional energy. The connection continues, but in a negative fashion.

The ties that bind us together not only have lasting strength, but also reach both back through the generations and forward for many years to come. Each generation inherits values, beliefs and ideas about what's admirable and what's possible, and learns important life skills from those who came before. Our parents give us language, ethnic and spiritual practices, their own and/or their ancestors' migration stories, a starting point for socioeconomic class, and expectations about education and the world of work. They offer these gifts through what they tell us, but even more importantly through what they show us. Those near to our parents—extended family, friends and community members—contribute as well. Everyone adds to the mix, reshaping legacies, inventing new ones, and passing it all forward. In this way we continue the stories of our families. We're doing this today and every day.

Our actions during our child's early years make a crucial contribution, of course, because this is their most formative time. At this book's opening I quoted my friend and family therapy mentor Monica McGoldrick, who said, "Think about how you want your kids to remember this time 20 years from now." Her words remind us that our child watches and absorbs, and, from age 4 or so, she or he *remembers*. The way we care for our child, the home and community we provide, and the way we live our own lives make a defining impact.

If you are a new parent, I invite you to imagine that time years from now when sleepless nights, toilet training, first grade, first dates and many graduations have passed, and your child, unimaginably, is a young adult. That day will come more quickly than you may imagine, for, as you have undoubtedly heard, the early days of parenting can feel endless but the years seem to gallop by. I ask you to imagine that time many years from now because what you do today—this very day—will help shape where you and your child find yourselves then.

Monica's words are not just for new parents but for the rest of us as well, because parenting *never* ends. No matter our age, we get the opportunity to shine as role models for our children (and perhaps our children's children) when we consistently show them affection, respect and encouragement even when we don't understand or agree with their choices, when we say no to them and hold our ground with love and firmness rather than hostility, and when we show them that the conflicts that will inevitably arise between us need not be avoided but can, instead, be faced with an open heart and, ultimately, bring us closer together.

Much of what we do in the days and years ahead, even when not directly involving our children, will nonetheless make a lasting impression upon them. Will we follow our own dreams, embracing the fullness of life for ourselves and showing them that their own adulthood can become a similarly rewarding adventure? Will we face up to our personal difficulties and ask for help when we need it even when our challenges involve addiction, mental health problems or other concerns that have been stigmatized? Will we do all that we can to care for our communities, and the planet upon which each of us depends? Will we greet the inevitable losses ahead with openness and grace, showing by our example that grief, the cost of having loved, will not destroy us but, on the contrary, help us heal? I hope this book will help you follow through.

Today, you and I are building legacies of our own as we face new challenges, move through them with all the courage and grace we can muster, and, hopefully, grow a bit wiser. We add to our life stories every day, all the while sharing them with those closest to us. Here's hoping that your story, the one you give to your child, is filled with love, health, success and joy.

Author's Gratitude

I'm grateful to Laura Mann, who suggested that I write this book. It wouldn't have happened otherwise.

Brad Harrington, Jorge Petit, and Lloyd Sederer read the manuscript, offered helpful comments, and wrote endorsements for the book. I thank them for the generous gift of their time and wisdom.

Longtime friends Monica McGoldrick and Lynn Parker showed me the same kindness. They critiqued the manuscript and wrote words of praise. Monica's renown as a family therapist and educator drew me to her training institute more than 25 years ago. It was one of the best decisions I've made. Lynn is another of my family therapy mentors and a dear friend. We've written, laughed and cried together.

Marian Sandmaier edited the manuscript, bettering it in a number of ways. I'm grateful to Marian and to Jackie Hudak for introducing me to her.

Wendy Brennan has been a collaborator on many projects and a cheerleader for all of my efforts. For me, she's one of those rare people we recognize immediately as a kindred spirit, perhaps one with whom we've walked in other times.

Barbara Ricci, a brilliant community organizer and leader in the world of business, has given me great support and encouragement. I'm grateful to have her in my corner.

Rich Rassmann, my journalist friend, corrected punctuation and made other valuable recommendations that polished the text— and he did it all in one weekend. Amazing.

Ken Dolan-Del Vecchio

Shirley Cresci, Vince Browne, Andy and Nita Crighton, Mike DiMaio, Sharon Dumont, Roy Freiman, Lucille Grey, and Gloria McDonald read the manuscript and gave helpful criticism. Shirley, Mike, Roy, and Lucille also allowed me to feature them, undisguised, in the text.

My permaculture coach, Jonathan Bates, is helping me create my greener future. He also graciously agreed to be featured in the book.

I'm grateful to Norbert Brau, Mariam Banafti, Julie Bukar, Tarik Cherkaoui, Celinda English, Andy Germak, Marie Hitchman, Hyan Im, Rick Keshishian, Theresa Messineo, and Paul Zeller. They exemplify all that friendship has to offer.

My gratitude and empathy for my parents, Barbara and Joseph Del Vecchio, grows with each passing year. They strove to be exceptional parents and, of course, were imperfect human beings like the rest of us. Now well into their next journeys, I hold their spirits close.

Lynn Dolan, my former spouse and my son's mother, was one of the first people to read an early draft. She gave immensely insightful recommendations. Now enjoying world travel and the other joys of semi-retirement, she has long been one of my most valued role models. I am grateful that we are family.

I thank my closest friends, David Drummond and Sterling McAndrew, who hosted me at their home in the Pennsylvania countryside on several "writing weekends." David introduced me to the man who would become my husband.

Several months ago, I visited my son, Erik, then 24 and sharing a home in Germany with his girlfriend, Christina Hilger. As they welcomed me into their apartment I felt jolted into the awareness that my child had become a fully-fledged adult. A more thoughtful, intelligent and kind young man would be difficult to find. He is a brilliant light in my life. A professional writer, Erik gave me recommendations that tightened the book's focus. Christina radiates warmth and kindness. A student of interior architecture, she is

174

also an accomplished artist. Christina's painting adorns the book's cover. (Christina and Erik got married last month and Christina now shares our last name.)

Tim Garrett, my husband, showers me with love, under-standing and encouragement. He's also a superb writer. Fortune smiled upon me the day David introduced us 19 years ago.

About the Author

Ken Dolan-Del Vecchio is a family therapist, author, speaker, and corporate health and wellness leader with over 25 years' experience in the arena of personal, family, organizational and community empowerment. He is a Licensed Marriage Family and Therapist (LMFT), Licensed Clinical Social Worker (LCSW) and Senior Professional in Human Resources (SPHR). Ken earned his B.A. in biopsychology at Cornell University and Master of Social Work (MSW) at Hunter College of the City University of New York. He completed a three-year post-graduate program in family therapy at The Multicultural Family Institute in Highland Park, New Jersey, where he now serves on the board of directors.

A nationally recognized expert on mental health and the workplace, Ken has been featured in a variety of broadcast and print media, notably *The Wall Street Journal*, *Reuters*, *Smart Money*, and *Fox Business News*. He has written scholarly articles and chapters in family therapy texts on social justice-based psychotherapy. Ken has authored four books, including *Making Love, Playing Power: Men, Women, and the Rewards of Intimate Justice* and *The Pet Loss Companion: Healing Advice from Family Therapists Who Lead Pet Loss Groups.*

Ken recently retired from his role as Vice President, Health and Wellness, at Prudential Financial, where he was responsible for behavioral health services for the company's 20,000 domestic employees, as well as organizational consultation and training on leadership, interpersonal skills, and performance management. While at Prudential, Ken was recognized as the 2016 Corporate Leader of the Year by the National Alliance on Mental Illness' NYC-Metro Chapter. His team's work led to Prudential receiving the American Psychological Association's 2017 Award for Organizational Excellence. Also in 2017, Ken was given the Annual Leadership Award from EASNA, The Employee Assistance Trade Association.

Ken recently founded GreenGate Leadership, LLC, the company for which he provides coaching and consultation for organizational leaders, as well as keynotes on exceptional parenting, healthy relationships, leadership skills; diversity, power and privilege in the workplace; and workplace violence prevention. He speaks regularly at corporations, professional conferences, universities, government agencies, and community events.

Learn more at www.greengateleadership.com.